The Witches' Almanac

Spring 2007 — Spring 2008

CONTAINING pictorial and explicit delineations of the
magical phases of the Moon together with information about astrological
portents of the year to come and various aspects of occult knowledge
enabling all who read to improve their lives in the old manner.

The Witches' Almanac, Ltd.

Publishers   Newport, Rhode Island
www.TheWitchesAlmanac.com

Address all inquiries and information to
THE WITCHES' ALMANAC, LTD.
P.O. Box 1292
Newport, RI 02840-9998

10-ISBN: 0-9773703-0-5
13-ISBN: 978-0-9773703-0-6

ISSN: 1522-3183

First Printing September 2006

Printed in the United States of America

Established 1971 by Elizabeth Pepper

Preface

This year we dedicate *The Witches' Almanac* to the element of Water. The dream world, sometimes known as the water world, is a place of mystery, illusion and the unknown. What is real? What is not? Although most people find this world challenging, a few embrace its secrets and power.

The mundane world has its temptations, among them passions, pleasures of the senses and ego. The realm of the Water element has its lure as well, for it is a place of introspection. Here we learn the craft of making our dreams real. But we often lose a sense of security when the familiar world and our ego recede for the opportunity to perceive the mysterious. There seems less to hold on to as we lose our tight grip of the reality we hold so dear.

This is when our magical senses begin to take hold of us. We see with magic eyes and we hear with magic ears; the world around us becomes alive with a presence of enchantment. This doesn't mean that we don't feel secure in this place. Rather our sense of safety is based on something other than the positive reinforcement we receive from our environment. Our security begins to become stronger from within ourselves. What could be better? For this is all that we have control over. This is the true inner strength, vital for all who engage in metaphysical studies.

The river can flow or run dry. Sensitivity, psychic talents, visions, intuition or dreamscapes can either overwhelm us or be nonexistent in our lives. The wise person knows how to develop these talents and balance them within. With these thoughts in mind, we welcome you to this Water-issue Almanac and its pages to inspire your imagination and dreams.

HOLIDAYS

Spring 2007 to Spring 2008

✳

Astrologer   Dikki-Jo Mullen
Climatologist   Tom C. Lang
Production Consultant   Robin Antoni
Art Director   Karen Marks
Research   Susan Chaunt
Sales   Ellen Lynch
Shipping, Bookkeeping   Doreen Bullock

CONTENTS

ANDREW THEITIC – Executive Editor

BARBARA STACY, JEAN MARIE WALSH
Associate Editors

The Wild Swans at Coole

The trees are in their autumn beauty,
The woodland paths are dry,
Under the October twilight the water
Mirrors a still sky;
Upon the brimming water among the stones
Are nine and fifty swans.

The nineteenth Autumn has come upon me
Since I first made my count;
I saw, before I had well finished,
All suddenly mount
And scatter wheeling in great broken rings
Upon their clamorous wings.

I have looked upon those brilliant creatures,
And now my heart is sore.
All's changed since I, hearing at twilight,
The first time on this shore,
The bell-beat of their wings above my head,
Trod with a lighter tread.

Unwearied still, lover by lover,
They paddle in the cold,
Companionable streams or climb the air;
Their hearts have not grown old;
Passion or conquest, wander where they will,
Attend upon them still.

But now they drift on the still water
Mysterious, beautiful;
Among what rushes will they build,
By what lake's edge or pool
Delight men's eyes,
When I awake some day
To find they have flown away?

–WILLIAM BUTLER YEATS

Yesterday, Today and Tomorrow

by Herb McSidhe

CAVE OF BASQUE WITCHES. The world of Basque witchery derives from remote times and is still celebrated at the Akelarre, literally "field of the he-goats." A cave at the site was hosted of old, locals believe, by the devil in  the form of a goat. On August 15, the fourth day of patron festivals, elderly locals gather in a cavern called "the cave of the witches." They bring a ram inside and roast it. "At noon the old of the town gather and the meat is eaten with bread and wine," José Miguel of Barandiarán assures us. Later they perform a dance in the town plaza. But how did the ancient witches celebrate? Some experts claim that what we "know" are fantasies, evolved from the malevolent minds of Inquisitors. The tribunal "revealed" that the witches glided in on the backs of animals, sometimes becoming the animals themselves. Neophytes were presented, witches made confessions, and in front of fires plunged into dance accompanied by little drums, and also accompanied by alcohol and hallucinogens. The gathering ended with a tremendous din at rooster crow.

BYE, BYE, BIRDIES. For more than 300 years, ravens have resided at the Tower of London. During the seventeenth century, King Charles II decreed that at least six ravens were to be kept at all times to protect the kingdom. But in view of the spread of bird flu throughout Europe, the Tower Raven Master decided in February '06 it was time to bring the world's most famous birds indoors. It was feared that the royal ravens risked mingling with a wild flock and the disease might spread to Britain. For now Baldrick, Branwen, Gwyllum, Hugine, Munin and Thor (have birds ever sounded so frightfully Anglo-Saxon?) will remain Tower denizens, but in a light, airy room.

DOCTORS LAUD HARRY POTTER. Researchers from the *British Medical Journal* tell us that the boy wizard can cast a spell on children that protects them from accident injuries. Consultant Keith Willett and surgeon Stephen Gwilym, working a weekend shift at a hospital in Oxford, noticed that the ward was oddly quiet on certain dates in summers. No flurry of the usual injuries from summer sports. Acting on a hunch

 provided by the behavior of Dr. Willett's son, they checked out statistics on when the new Rowling books were released. The doctors studied the number of seven- to fifteen-year-olds admitted to emergency over a three-year period on two significant days – times when a new Harry Potter book was released. For June and July weekends without any particular literary thrills for kids, an average of 67 percent of hospital admissions were children. When a new Rowling book hit the bookstores, figures dropped to 36 or 37 percent. Mothers will be happy to hear that the majority of kids opted to stay home and read about Quidditch, the magical sport, rather than being clobbered by soccer balls, plummeting from trees or falling off bikes. "Harry Potter books seem to protect children from traumatic injuries," stated Gwilym.

LESTAT, C'EST BLAH. Anne Rice's literary creation, *Lestat*, arose on Broadway in April 2006 and expired a month later. The lavish musical was based on Rice's blockbuster *Vampire Chronicles*. Sir Elton John provided the music and the combination of talents seemed to be a theatrical marriage made in heaven. *Lestat* was nominated for two Tony awards, and according to Rice the pre-Broadway run at the Curran Theater grossed a record-breaking $4,315,293. What went wrong? Just about everything, including a neck-bite review by Ben Brantley, the heavyweight critic at *The New York Times*. The column mayhem began, "A promising new contender has arrived in a crowded pharmaceutical field. Joining the ranks of Ambien, Lunesta, Sonata and other prescription lullaby drugs is *Lestat*, the musical sleeping pill that opened last night at the Palace Theater." The review went downhill from there, and John may still be cringing.

IN SEARCH OF REBECCA NURSE. Archaeology students at Phillips Academy in Andover, Mass., will take part in the first dig at the historic home of Rebecca Nurse. In 1692, during the Salem witchcraft trials, the 71-year-old woman faced accusers and was found innocent But after the verdict, the girls who accused Nurse and others of witchcraft experienced terrifying torments. The judge urged the jury to reconsider its decision, the verdict was reversed, and Nurse was hanged. At that time bodies of such pariahs were considered not fit for Christian burial and flung into shallow graves. But legend has it that the Nurse family rescued Rebecca from the ditch

in Salem and buried her on the family estate in what is now Danvers, Mass. "The likelihood of the students finding her remains are slim," declares Glenn Mairo, a volunteer at the Rebecca Nurse Homestead. During the seventeenth century the property extended to 300 acres; now it has dwindled to 27 acres. Nevertheless the kids are digging away, and found objects will be displayed at the Rebecca Nurse Homestead.

Turkey

CROESUS GOLD. An ancient gold brooch of a winged horse and a gold coin, treasures of King Croesus, have been backing and forthing from the Metropolitan Museum in New York to the Usak Museum in western Turkey. The pieces, priceless artifacts from the fifth century B.C., were part of a display plundered from the Usak that wound up at the Met. After a long legal battle, the treasures were returned to Turkey. Now Atilla Koc, Turkey's culture minister, states in the Milliyet newspaper that the Croesus pieces have been stolen yet again and switched with replicas. Where has the flying horse flown? We hope the answer won't cause red faces in the U.S.

WE SEEK HIM HERE, WE SEEK HIM THERE. Consider the pleasures and perils of invisibility. The mind-boggling theory seems on its way to reality, according to science researchers. They tell us that creating such spooky concealment is an attainable goal by means of a cloak of manmade material unlike anything in nature. Labs are working on such a substance. Andrew Bridges reports in *The Miami Herald*, "Like a river streaming around a smooth boulder, light and all other forms of electromagnetic radiation would strike the cloak and simply flow around it, continuing on as if it had never bumped up against an obstacle. This would give an onlooker the apparent ability to peer right through the cloak, with everything tucked inside concealed from view." Patanjali Parimi, a physicist and design engineer at Northeastern University, assures us that we will have an invisibility cloak "after not too long," and another physicist mentions eighteen months. No statement from the folks at Hogwarts.

ZIMBABWE DITHERS ABOUT WITCHES. Do they want them or don't they? Zimbabweans reflect changing views according to shifting political winds. Early in 2006 the government issued the Witchcraft Suppression Act, making the practice a criminal offense punishable by a five-year jail term or fine. The new law also made it illegal to hire a witch or assist in the practice of

witchcraft, but the decree also provided protection for people "groundlessly" accused of witchcraft. To many Zimbabweans, especially those in rural  areas, the legislation seemed to proclaim an absurdity – that supernatural powers do not exist. To address the uproar, in July the government issued a new law. It conceded that supernatural powers do exist, but that such powers may not be used to cause harm. Judge Custom Kachambwa pointed out that the law will not be easy to administer. Defendants may be traditional healers who could be accused of practicing harmful magic should a patient fail to recover. However the situation plays out, the country (formerly Rhodesia) signals a move away from colonial Western culture and chooses to embrace its own ancient traditions.

WICKED IN WICKER. Since the American remake of *The Wicker Man* and two recent books about the film, interest has revived in the English classic. The American remake by Neil LaBute, starring Nicolas Cage, has outraged the original artists, including Christopher Lee and director Robin Hardy. And you know how Lee gets when he is annoyed. The plot of the 1973 version: A child has gone missing and Sergeant Neil Howie (Edward Woodward) is investigating. He learns that the townspeople follow a neo-pagan religion led by Lord Summerisle, played by Lee with marvelously chilly charm. Howie, a devout Christian, is shocked by the islanders' bizarre rituals – including Willow (Britt Eklund), dancing in the buff and giving it her all. The sound track is beautiful, many of the pieces Irish and Scottish folk songs. Of course a terrifying Wicker Man turns up, a giant effigy made to burn in a sinister purpose. The plot is enormously suspenseful, twisting and turning, and we won't give away the story. The movie has often been listed erroneously as a horror film, but it is miles removed from bash-and-slash junk and is more accurately classified as a dark drama – although the history of its release is kind of a horror story. Unappreciated by its own producers, the superb movie was butchered in the cutting and opened as the flip side of a double bill. Nonetheless critics loved it and as for any outstanding movie, friends tell friends. The original *Wicker Man* has taken on a giant step of its own and become a cult classic.

THE BASQUE MYSTIQUE

The Lauburu, *a Basque cultural icon*

"BEFORE GOD was God and boulders were boulders, Basques were already Basques" is a popular saying referring to one of the world's most ancient civilizations. The name "Basque" derives from a term meaning "wild tribes." For more than seven thousand years, against all odds, the Basques have fiercely retained their unique identity and maintained a free spirit. Linguists agree that the Basque language, Euskara, is unlike any other tongue on earth. It is so impossibly complex that outsiders claim even the devil couldn't learn it.

The Basque country spans a hundred mile stretch from Bilboa, Spain, to Bayonne, France, insulated from the rest of Europe by the Pyrenees mountains and the Bay of Biscay on the Atlantic coast. The anthropologist José Miguel de Barandiarán assures us that blood typing and other genetic studies indicate that the Basque people are as unique as their language. They are physically unlike any other race and may be a remainder of early Stone Age civilizations. Comparisons between the bones of a Cro-Magnon man with those of a contemporary Basque show amazing similarities.

We know little about ancient Basque beliefs, but what we know is vivid. In the beginning a great fire serpent lived in the earth; he uncoiled to become the Pyrenees mountains. From his seven gaping jaws the Basques were born. During the sixteenth century, a few books were published in Euskara that preserved parts of the Basque's magical pagan and ancient oral tradition. The people believed in a universal god, Yaun-Goicoa, who created three life forces: *Egia*, the light of the spirit; *Ekhia*, the sun, the light of the world; and *Begia*, the eye, the light of the body. The cosmogony also included a supreme goddess, Mari, and her consort Sugaar. She assumed many forms, sometimes as women, sometimes as a red animal, sometimes as a black goat, among others. But Sugaar was always depicted either as a man or a dragon. Mari was served by the Sorginak, legendary creatures similar to pagan priestesses or witches. Their kingdom was chthonic, as all its characters abide on earth or below it. The sky was conceived as a virtual empty passageway through which divinities range and herd clouds.

We have other slim clues to archaic divinities. A prehistoric altar carried an inscription to Erditse, a maternity goddess. Pagans among the Basques also told of Tartalo. He was a one-eyed giant, a Cyclops-like hunter and shepherd, whose spirit haunts remote mountain paths.

Despite its daunting borders, the Basque region has experienced a long line of would-be conquerors, from the Celts and Romans to the Arabs and French. The ETA organization, acronym for Basque Country Freedom in Euskara, was active at the end of the last century to defend the region against a coup by the Fascist General Franco. In 1937 the town of Guernica was bombed, memorialized by the Picasso masterpiece.

The Basques were finally united in three separate provinces under their own flag in 1980. A movement persists to restore autonomy as a separate nation. The Euskara language, which had been dying out, is being revived. Euskara appears, along with Spanish and French, as an official language on street signs and public documents.

Basques turn up everywhere. They have emigrated to the USA, Argentina, Chile and Mexico in large numbers. Key Biscayne and Biscayne Bay in Florida were named by Basque immigrants in honor of their homeland. Jai Alai ("happy game" in Euskara) is a Basque tradition with fans of the fast handball game everywhere.

The Basque region has prospered, much of it thanks to tourism. The resort town of San Sebastian was popularized by Spain's Queen Isabel II in 1845. The ailing queen was dispatched to the site by a doctor, and the sea air and delectable seafood worked their magic.

Today travelers from around the world visit the Basque region. The country is the site of an international film festival and offers jazz festivals, regattas, and theaters. Concerts feature Basque music of brilliance and charm, and tales of a witches' sabbat are hinted at in the lyrics of the oldest local ballads. Masquerades, plays, riddles and Mundaka, a sensual dance, also feature mystical elements with origins lost in time. During April, coinciding with Easter and the vernal equinox, the timeless mystical themes are offered in public performances. And who knows? While exploring the region's limestone caves you may encounter the Laminak, legendary fairies of beautiful underground castles. If legendary they are.

– ESTHER ELAYNE

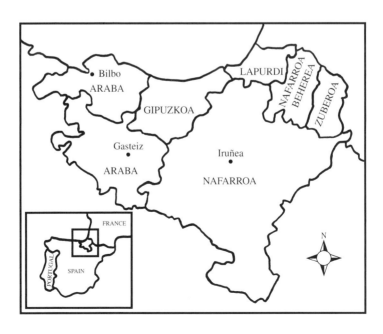

Spring Egg Spells

THE HARE, not the fuzzy bunny of cards and decorations, has long been a symbol of fertility. The hare excels at reproduction and provides an impressive number of offspring in a speedy mode. Since ancient times eggs also represented new life, welcome by implication. Children were essential to family survival, sharing the backbreaking work of farming. But symbols extolling human fertility were less enthusiastically viewed after the Industrial Revolution. With the prevalence of factories, the offspring of city-dwellers were now more liability than asset, especially after the law prevented child labor.

But the use of fertility symbols survives. Faced with the desire for children, some people continue to use eggs in rituals to aid conception. Some modern pagans and witches make use of symbols not as literal aids of physical reproduction, but to focus on the fecundity of mind, spirit, and the land. Many look upon spring and the humble Ostara Egg as yet another method of spell-work. Using magical correspondences, witches color and decorate eggs according to a wish or desire to be manifested. Choosing egg colors appropriate for your intention works similarly to choosing candle colors – the correspondences are generally the same. For example, many people choose red for healing because red is the color of blood, and blood represents vitality. The ancient Chinese opted for red eggs. Others choose green because it is the color of growing things, and growth of new cells is important in healing. Some prefer pink, the hue of healthy cheeks in light skin color, the source of the expression "in the pink" to describe good health. Those who use the yogic chakra system might select pink because it is associated with the heart chakra. The heart, or self-love, is often considered necessary for healing.

If you colored eggs as a child, you probably boiled them or tapped a small hole in each end and blew out the contents. But for magical spells you want raw eggs with the contents intact. Fertilized eggs, available in health-food stores or from farms, are better for spells than unfertilized commercial eggs. For best coloring results, start with a white egg, although brown eggs will do. Some chickens lay colored eggs. The Auracana chicken lays blue or green eggs, and you may be lucky enough to find eggs in the natural color needed for your spell.

Ritual preparations

To prepare the egg for coloring, wipe it with white vinegar or dip it in a solution of white vinegar and water; rinse with water. This makes the surface of the egg more porous, which helps it absorb the dye. For dye, use standard food coloring, available year-around in the baking section of your local grocery, or use an Easter egg kit. You can even use colored markers and crayons to avoid dye altogether. But for more authentic magical eggs, choose natural food coloring with dyes from nature.

For red, use the juice of raspberries, cranberries or blackberries. If you can't find fresh berries, look for frozen berries in the freezer section.

For pink, use beet juice and vinegar, the juice of pickled beets or red grape juice.

For green, a handful of carrot tops or spinach leaves yield a pale yellow-green.

For yellow, a color often used for spells regarding success, try ground turmeric.

For dark blue, the color associated with expansive Jupiter, slice red cabbage thinly and cover with water in a non-aluminum pot. (Because this color can stain, it's best to use a dark enamel pot or an old pot you don't care about.) Boil until tender. Pour into a jar, add the egg and leave overnight.

Drawing the magical symbols

You can add magical symbols after you color, using your choice of marker, paints, colored pens or whatever you choose. Or use crayons before you color, then remove the wax with a paper towel dipped in hot water.

For success, draw an icon of the sun or your hope of success. For example, for successful completion of a college degree, draw a diploma scroll or write the actual words that will be on your diploma.

For health, you may draw the staff of Aesclepias, the Greco-Roman god of medicine, a staff with a single snake twined around it.

For love, self-love or otherwise, decorate your pink egg with heart symbols and the word "love" in your own language or in all languages you can find.

For prosperity, use the sign of your local currency: a dollar sign, a pound sign, the euro sign, and so on.

Use your imagination. Draw whatever symbolizes your intention. After your egg is dry, find an appropriate place for burial, perhaps a site near your house or where you walk frequently. Or use a flowerpot filled with rich soil; you may want to decorate the pot with appropriate colors and symbols. Hold the egg in both hands, send your intent into the egg and bury it as you would a seed.

– MORVEN WESTFIELD

FREEMASONRY

THE FIRST GRAND LODGE of Free-masonry was formed in 1717, and it is the oldest and largest fraternal society in the world. Although its origins will never be known definitively, some historians trace its start to the stone workers and master masons who built the great cathedrals of Europe. Some scholars say that the roots of Freema-sonry derive from the time of King Solomon during the construction of the great Temple of Jerusalem. Yet others tie the beginning of this ancient order to the Christian organization known as the Knights Templar.

The Templars were formed by the papal seat during the Crusades, approx-imately 1097 CE, to defend pilgrims vis-iting the Holy Land. As both a religious order and a military body, the Knights took up arms in the name of the Holy Roman Church. Although Freemasonry is not a religion, many Christian prin-ciples are important to the organization. No atheist, for instance, can be a Free-mason. All must share a belief in a single supreme being, although the term may be defined by the individual and not by the Masonic organization.

A Masonic sign composed of eight subsidiary signs, from a French calendar

The Knights Templar was a monas-tic order formed at the end of the first century. Although adherents began with little support or money, they somehow amassed great wealth increased by money lending. Some date the Free-masons' founding to 1307 in Scotland, where the Knights Templar retreated following a massacre in France. The Templars wished to ensure the sur-vival of their order under the guise of a secret society. Their downfall in France resulted from Pope Clem-ent V's support of King Philip IV of France. The French king then ordered the arrests of all known Templars on charges of heresy and of secret meet-ings and rituals. Following the arrests, trials and executions, the state seized Templar assets and lands.

Masons share a system of morality expressed through their symbols and allegory. The concepts of charity and light, as seen through the Mason's eyes, are paramount. The hidden meanings behind the pervasive sym-bols of the square, compasses and Bible provide three great Masonic lights in Christian countries. Else-where the appropriate tome of reli-gious law substitutes for the Bible. Charity is an important concept. Masons donate millions of dollars each year to the underprivileged, espe-cially to the support of ill children.

Ritual is an intrinsic part of the Freemasons' structure. Although many historians believe the Masonic rituals to be of ancient origin, others assert that they have developed over the centuries by a combination of various traditions. Some Masons believe that the symbols of Freemasonry stem from a time before King Solomon's Temple, and reach back to the great ancient culture of Egypt. Yet as a practice, Freemasonry revolves around the all-encompassing mythology which features King Solomon's Temple in Jerusalem as its central theme.

One unique method of teaching the mysteries is through the use of the ritual play. The enactment of a drama by lodge members, based on the symbology of the order, brings a clearer understanding to the initiate.

The followers of Freemasonry have always insisted on secrecy. A variety of passwords and hand grips are an integral part of the Masonic rituals. The original use of secrecy was probably intended to help the stonemasons of the time recognize their own kind when they were in need of help. To a non-initiate, the oath of initiation would certainly seem frightening. The oath is used to continue the age-old tradition of secrecy. When the secrecy is broken, the symbols which represent the mysteries are subject to ridicule by the unenlightened.

The various traditions of Freemasonry are a blend of contrived legend and historical fact, perhaps going back to the eighteenth century when lodges began to accept members that were not stonemasons. Today the term "operative" refers to a practicing stonemason and term "speculative" refers to a figurative stonemason – one who deals in the concepts of Freemasonry.

For Freemasons, ancient lore is of great importance to their craft. The time-honored legends surrounding King Solomon's Temple are probably the most significant of all. The probability is that this is the first time that we see divinity exemplified by a temple constructed by human hands. As a result, geometry has become known as a sacred science. King Solomon's Temple was believed to have been constructed under the watchful eye of the priests guarding the sacred mysteries. As knowledge spread across Europe, mystery schools sprang up in all countries. Masons were charged with the construction of all sacred temples and churches, and therefore influenced by all the mystery religions. The Brotherhood of Freemasonry exemplifies the chief modern form of ancient mysteries.

An amazing variety of men have taken the Masonic oath of secrecy:

Irving Berlin, W.C. Fields, Henry Ford, Frederick the Great, Benjamin Franklin, Clark Gable, John Glenn, Rudyard Kipling, General Douglas MacArthur, Dr. Charles Mayo, Dr. Mesmer, Wolfgang Amadeus Mozart, Paul Revere, the Ringling Brothers, Red Skelton, Danny Thomas, John Wayne.

A comprehensive list may be found at http://www.masonicinfo.com/famous1.htm

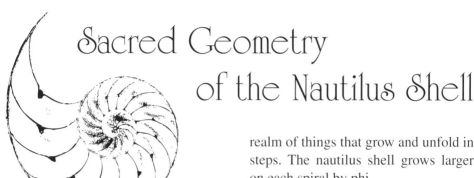

Sacred Geometry of the Nautilus Shell

The Chambered Nautilus

The chambered nautilus is a living fossil that has survived in oceans for the last five hundred million years, existing before fish, dinosaurs or mammals. Once much larger, today's mollusk measures about 10 inches, and can be found on the slopes of deep reefs in the Indian and Pacific oceans. The nautiluses hatch from eggs after twelve months with their shells already consisting of four chambers. Their large snail-like shells coil upwards, lined with mother-of-pearl. The mollusks mature slowly and live for up to sixteen years. As the shell grows, it subdivides into as many as thirty chambers. The body moves forward into the new larger chamber and produces a wall to seal off the older chamber. The empty chambers regulate buoyancy. A cross-section of the nautilus shell shows the cycles of its growth as a series of chambers arranged in a precise Golden Mean spiral.

The Golden Mean is represented by the Greek letter phi (the decimal representation of 1.6180...), one of those mysterious natural numbers that seems to arise from the basic structure of our cosmos. Phi appears regularly in the realm of things that grow and unfold in steps. The nautilus shell grows larger on each spiral by phi.

With each revolution completing a cycle of evolution, the Golden Mean spiral is symbolic of life's unfolding mysteries. The continuous curves of the spirals, feminine in nature, and the ratios between each of the chambers reveal the intimate relationship between the harmonics of nature and "Sacred Geometry," the term used to describe the basic building blocks of the universe.

An ancient science

This ancient science explores and explains the physical and energy patterns that create and unify all things and reveals the way that the universe of creation organizes itself. Every natural pattern of growth or movement conforms inevitably to one or more geometric shapes. From the molecules of our DNA to the galaxy we spiral within, life and its forms emerge from geometric codes. Egyptians were the earliest known masters of Sacred Geometry. They embedded its secrets in the ground plans of their temples, their frescoes and in the Giza pyramid. Although these enlightened people used geometry for terrestrial applications – the root of "geo-metry" is "measure of the earth," – the aim was metaphysical in nature.

Sacred Geometry reflects the universe, its pure forms and the dynamic

relationship of our selves to nature – the inseparable relationship of the part to the whole. By studying the Sacred Geometry of one thing, we give meaning and structural insight into the workings of the inner self. As the renowned geometer Robert Lawlor observes, "The implicit goal of this education was to enable the mind to become a channel through which the 'earth' (the level of manifested form) could receive the abstract, cosmic life of the heavens. The practice of geometry was an approach to the way in which the universe is ordered and sustained. Geometric diagrams can be contemplated as still moments revealing a continuous, timeless, universal action generally hidden from our sensory perception. Thus a seemingly common mathematical activity can become a discipline for intellectual and spiritual insight."

Phi, the Golden Ratio

The spiral is a common element of Sacred Geometry as well as to all natural development. Spirals in nature tend to follow the Golden Ratio (phi) or Fibonacci Sequence in their rates of expansion. The key to Sacred Geometry is the relationship between the progression of growth and proportion. Harmonic proportion and progression are the essence of the created universe and are consistent with nature around us. The natural progression follows a series that is popularized in the West as the "Fibonacci Series," where the first two numbers in the series are added to create the third number, for a series of numbers that

begins 0, 1, 1, 2, 3, 5, 8, 13, 21, 34, 55, 89, 144, 233, 377, 610, 987… and goes on ad infinitum. The ratio of the numbers gains great importance as the series continues. By dividing one number by the previous number, the answers result in or come closer to phi: 3/5 = 1.6666, 13/8 = 1.6250, 233/144 = 1.6180.

These numbers can be demonstrated with the spiral of the nautilus. Beginning with a small single square (one unit per side), continue adding larger and larger squares in a counterclockwise direction using the following number sequence: 1, 1, 2, 3, 5, 8, 13… as illustrated.

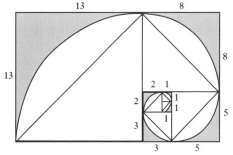

Draw diagonals through every square in a counterclockwise direction. Using the diagonals as guides, draw a smooth spiraling curve from the smallest one-unit square outward through your largest square. The proportional relationship of the squares quickly begins to approach the Golden Proportion of 1:1.618… phi.

The Golden Ratio (phi) is the unique ratio such that the ratio of the whole to the larger portion is the same as the ratio of the larger portion to the smaller portion. The ratio links each chamber of the nautilus to the new growth and symbolically, each new generation to its ancestors, preserving the continuity of relationship as the means for retracing its lineage.

This geometry of the nautilus can be found in the spiral patterns of cauliflower, the placement of the leaves on most plants, the arrangement of pattern on a pine cone. The ratios can be retrieved from the shape of our DNA and the measurement of distant galaxies as the Sacred Geometry demonstrates the blueprint of the sacred foundation of all things and the interconnectedness of all the various parts of the whole.

– MARSHA BARD

Meditation on the Spirals of the Nautilus

If you are fortunate enough to have a cross-section of a nautilus shell, hold it in your hands. If you don't have the actual shell, a picture of a cross-section of the shell will be an acceptable substitute. Quiet your thoughts. For a moment, just concentrate on the beginning point of the spiral deep within the shell. With your eyes open, follow the spiral around and around as it climbs higher and higher, like a staircase, opening into larger and larger chambers.

Close your eyes and visualize that central point again and imagine yourself, very small, at the beginning of the spiral. Just as you followed the spiral around and around like a staircase, imagine yourself climbing those stairs, spiraling around and around, climbing higher and higher and moving up and out through the chambers, each chamber being a larger replica of the one before. Go slowly and allow yourself to experience the turns of the spiral and how it gets wider and wider at each turn. In your mind's eye, look down into the spiral and view the center once again to see how far you have gone.

The spiral staircase can go anywhere you want it to go, or you can stop in any one of the chambers to receive the knowledge and wisdom of that chamber. Remember that the nautilus has been replicating itself for five hundred million years and carries in its chambers the memories and knowledge of times past.

When you feel that you have experienced the upward turning of the spiral, look back once again to the center to see how far you have climbed. Then relax your mind and rest for a time within the spiral's energy.

Open your eyes and be sure to write down any experiences or any knowledge you have received from the nautilus.

Illustration by Ogmios MacMerlin

YEAR OF THE BOAR
February 18, 2007 to February 6, 2008

The Boar symbolizes practicality combined with comfort. Its quest is creativity, especially regarding financial security. The boar is the twelfth and final Chinese zodiac sign. When Buddha invited the animals to his famous birthday party, each of the guests were gifted with a year. Boar was the last to arrive, and he forever dreads tardiness. Especially this year, be aware of time management and be on time for appointments.

People born during a Boar Year are beloved for their kindness, loyalty and sincerity; they find dishonesty hard to forgive. Courageous and headstrong, Boars often accomplish much and are seldom deterred once they set upon a course of action. Theirs is an adventurous nature. Since impulsiveness sometimes leads to regrets, the consequences must be considered beforehand. Although short of temper, Boars don't like arguments and tension. Their real preference is for creature comforts and serenity in beautiful, even opulent, surroundings. Good manners, good taste and classiness are cherished. In their innermost hearts Boars want all to be well and comfortable. These qualities should not be confused with snobbishness, they are simply ultimate refinement. If you were born during one of the Years of the Boar listed below, you will be starting a new cycle of growth and opportunity this year.

1911 1923 1935 1947 1959 1971 1983 1995 2007

Wine and the Ritual Libation

The magic of fermented crushed grapes has long been associated with courage, love, joy and longevity. The role of wine in ritual is one of thanksgiving. Such usage celebrates positive actions. The Roman gods Themis and Bacchus, the Egyptian deities Horus and Osiris as well as the Greek Dionysus and Mesopotamian Ishtar are especially associated with libation offerings of wine.

In King Tut's tomb the residue of a red wine was found, still preserved in sacred jars. In 121 BC the Roman Pliny

FIVE THOUSAND years ago, on the shores of the Mediterranean Sea, sailors sought the favor of the gods. To assure a safe voyage, bottles of fragrant, colorful liquid were poured on newly completed ships. The offerings must have been acceptable, because the custom has continued through the ages. As the centuries passed, the Egyptians, Greeks, Romans, Celts and Vikings launched a new vessel with a libation.

The term "libation" borrows from the name of Liber, a classical god. Libation means offering a deity wine or other liquid as a way of asking a favor or expressing gratitude. Libations are poured onto the ground or into the water from a chalice. The gift can be oil, holy water, tea, coffee or whiskey as well as wine. The term "christening" was coined in modern times, but the intent is the same. The sea gods are presented with a lovingly selected drink to request safe passage. Old Ironsides, the first American warship, was christened with a bottle of the best Madeira. To this day the U.S. Navy always selects a bottle of domestic wine to celebrate and bless a ship's maiden voyage.

Amphora. *A two-handled pottery jar with a narrow neck used by the ancient Greeks and Romans to carry liquids, especially wine and oil.*

developed the first classification system to rate wines. Today the variety of available wines and their presentation has evolved into an incredibly intricate art and science. A visit to a winery strikes a divine nerve connection. The earth, the grapes and the winemakers all weave a magical story of the industry's domestic progress. In 1985 there were 712 wineries, mostly in California and New York. Now there are at least four thousand, located in all fifty states.

Long ago, the wary would share a bottle of wine to assure that it hadn't been poisoned. As a symbol of trust, glasses were touched and a blessing invoked. The bell-like sound of the toast was thought to drive away evil spirits. Butter, vanilla, and grapefruit are some of the descriptive terms used to identify a wine's bouquet or fragrance. The color, varying from deepest red to rose and white, is admired as the precious liquid trickles down upon being swirled in a glass. In Germany the resulting rivulets are called "church windows," in Spain "tears," in the U.K. and USA they are known as "legs." The little streams are actually part of wine's complex phenomenon related to the surface tension, evaporation and alcohol content. A connoisseur may be able to judge a wine's worth on its legs alone.

The Latin word *vitae*, for life, is the root of the words vine, vintage and vineyard, hinting at wine's life-giving properties. Wassail, *glogg*, *sangria* and mulled wine are various names used around the world for wine teamed with herbs, spices, sugar, fruit, juices and served hot. *Sangria* comes from the Spanish word *sangre*, "blood" – another link between wine and vitality.

– MARINA BRYONY

Caribbean Witches' Sangria

Combine one bottle of sweet red wine with an equal amount of water, 1/2 cup brown sugar, three sliced oranges and one sliced lemon. Add 1 teaspoon each of allspice, cloves, nutmeg and two cinnamon sticks. Simmer gently for 3 hours. Strain and serve either hot or chilled.

Goddess of the Sweet Waters

THE WORLD over, when we encounter water, we encounter the embodiment of the feminine, of purification and of fertility. Water sustains our fragile lives in the wombs of our mothers before we come to each incarnation. Water is the agent by which we cleanse both the body and the soul.

In many traditions the archetype of a feminine deity reflects the holiness of water. In the Yoruba cultures of West Africa, the primordial importance of water is acknowledged and venerated through worship of Osun, the riverine orisa, or "deity." She is the owner of all rivers and all the sweet waters of the world, including water in the bloodstream and elsewhere in the body. In sacred geography, Osun's energy and character is embodied in the holy river bearing her name. The Osun River rises in Ekiti State of eastern Nigeria and flows westward through Osogbo, the center of Osun worship. This is also the home of her highest ranking priestess, the Iya Osun, Mother Osun.

Many women who want children pray to Osun as the owner of the holy waters. At the palace of the Atoaja

"king," in Osogbo, the shrine to Osun offers a pot of water considered medicine for all and especially efficacious in achieving pregnancy. Many devotees will stop by with an offering of kola nuts, which the Iya Osun will gladly offer to Osun, as well as a prayer for the hopeful mother to be.

In a traditional society, especially among the Yoruba, fertility remains not only a necessity, but a blessing. Children are not seen as a burden, but as a way in which we can come back to this Earth. The belief prevails that once you pass to the Otherworld, you will be born again through your own bloodline. In Osun, the barren woman finds an orisa who has experienced the same concern. According to her mythology, at one time Osun also was a barren woman. Only through divination, sacrifice and the use of her own waters was Osun able to realize her fertility.

Osun in the Yoruba Diaspora has kept her association with childbearing; in fact, her devotees are especially fertile and love to bear one child after another. Poems from Yorubaland praise Osun as the mother who nurtures her worshipers by treating them as her own children, suckling them at her breast. Adherents also extolled her as the mother who gives birth with frequency and ease.

In the rainy season, when the Osun River becomes pregnant with her healing waters and the fecundity of the earth is at it height, the annual festival to the deity takes place. Her priestess, the Iya Osun, and her earthly counterpart/partner, the Atoaja, take center stage to propitiate the goddess effectively When that happens, the whole town, in fact, all of Yorubland can be prosperous.

As well as the orisa of bodily fertility, Osun can impart monetary fruitfulness as readily as she does children. Again, we can look to the deity's praise poetry to understand her association with wealth. In many poems we encounter the tall, slender light-skinned beauty adorned with precious brass and carrying a beaded comb. In the Osun River we find the Yoruba monetary exchange, the cowrie shell. Osun's association with wealth so prevails that in the Diaspora people down on their luck pray to her for financial stability. Frequently the devotee seeking wealth will find a river and offer five copper coins and honey, one of Osun's favorite foods. In Osogbo a person in need of money brings gifts to her grove and offers them to the river for the deity's favors.

The cowrie shell lends itself to prophecy as well as exchange. The goddess is a seer through her association with cowries and her marriage to Orunmila, the orisa of divination. In this aspect Osun appears as a woman of knowledge, the first to perform a system of divination with sixteen cowries. And in some mythologies Osun performs divination in the home of the Orisa Orunmila when he is away.

Although Osun personifies the ultimate femininity, like all of her sister orisas she embodies power. It was Osun who descended to earth with sixteen other orisas to ready the world for mankind. Among the orisa that descended, Osun was the only female and was not to be trifled with:

*Ifá was divined for the 200
    Irunmole on the right hand side.*

*Ifá was divined for the 200 Irunmole
    on the left hand side.*

*They were the ones who constructed
    the road to Opa's sacred grove.*

*They were the ones who constructed
    the road to Oro's sacred grove.*

They would not consult Osun.

*They called the spirit of Egun,
    Egun would not come.*

*They called the spirit of Oro,
    Oro would not come.*

*They made a road to Ile Ife,
    but none would use it.*

*They made pounded yam,
    it was full of lumps.*

They made amala, it was too watery.

*Ifá was divined for Osun, owner of
    the beautiful wooden comb.*

*Who used her powers to confound the
    efforts of the Irunmole.*

They went to Olódùmarè.

*They told him they were unable to
complete their tasks.*

*Olódùmarè asked, "What of the only
woman amongst you?"*

He asked, "Did you respect her?"

They told him they did not consult her.

*Olódùmarè advised that they should
return and include Osun in their
decision.*

*They returned and showed proper
respect for Osun.*

*They called the spirit of Egun,
Egun came.*

*They called the spirit of Oro,
Oro came.*

People used the road to Ile Ife.

They made pounded yam, it was good.

They made amala, it was good.

We give our reverence to Osun.

The unseen mother at every gathering.

The poem proclaims that a single woman was confounding the efforts of all the Irunmole, the male deities. In the mythology, on their former descent to earth the chauvinistic Irunmole treated Osun as a kitchen slave, refusing to recognize her as an equal. When all their efforts failed, the Irunmole returned to heaven and consulted with the high god Olódùmarè. He proclaimed that without the consent of Osun, nothing would be accomplished. Not only was the goddess to be consulted, she was to be initiated into their mysteries. In Osun we have the embodiment of wealth, prosperity, love, beauty, elegance, sexuality, sensuality and a divinely sanctioned feminist.

Mo ke mogha lodo omi – I cry for deliverance through water! ASE!

– IFADOYIN SANGOMUYIWA

*Nigerian Priest to Sango and
Babalawo "Father of Secrets"*

Praise Poem for Osun

Osun, goddess with fantastic crown of peacock plumage
Goddess of the river
Resounding ocean waves
Overwhelming and big
Men run when Osun takes over the road
Mighty sea that cannot be held
Oh! Beloved mother, you pamper children with brass
Wise one, owner of brass who never sleeps
You live with wisdom and give it away freely
Osun please give me my own money
Do not bury my money in the sand
Oh! Thank you, dear mother!

MOON GARDENING

BY PHASE

Sow, transplant, bud and graft *Plow, cultivate, weed and reap*

NEW	First Quarter	FULL	Last Quarter	NEW
Plant above-ground crops with outside seeds, flowering annuals.	Plant above-ground crops with inside seeds.	Plant root crops, bulbs, biennials, perennials.		Do not plant.

BY PLACE IN THE ZODIAC

Fruitful Signs

Cancer—Most favorable planting time for all leafy crops bearing fruit above ground. Prune to encourage growth in Cancer.

Scorpio—Second only to Cancer, a Scorpion Moon promises good germination and swift growth. In Scorpio, prune for bud development.

Pisces—Planting in the last of the Watery Triad is especially effective for root growth.

Taurus—The best time to plant root crops is when the Moon is in the sign of the Bull.

Capricorn—The Earthy Goat Moon promotes the growth of rhizomes, bulbs, roots, tubers and stalks. Prune now to strengthen branches.

Libra—Airy Libra may be the least beneficial of the Fruitful Signs, but is excellent for planting flowers and vines.

Barren Signs

Leo—Foremost of the Barren Signs, the Lion Moon is the best time to effectively destroy weeds and pests. Cultivate and till the soil.

Gemini—Harvest in the Airy Twins; gather herbs and roots. Reap when the Moon is in a sign of Air or Fire to assure best storage.

Virgo—Plow, cultivate, and control weeds and pests when the moon is in Virgo.

Sagittarius—Plow and cultivate the soil or harvest under the Archer Moon. Prune now to discourage growth.

Aquarius—This dry sign of Air is perfect for ground cultivation, reaping crops, gathering roots and herbs. It is a good time to destroy weeds and pests.

Aries—Cultivate, weed, and prune to lessen growth. Gather herbs and roots for storage.

Consult our Moon Calendar pages for phase and place in the zodiac circle. The Moon remains in a sign for about two-and-a-half days. Match your gardening activity to the day that follows the Moon's entry into that zodiac sign.

The Gifts of Aradia

THE LEGEND OF ARADIA came to light just before the turn of the present century when Maddalena, an Italian witch, delivered to Charles G. Leland a manuscript called the *Vangelo della-Streghe,* or the Gospel of the Witches. Leland assumed the material had been set down from oral narration of tales and traditions reaching back to Etruscan times. Realizing his book *Aradia* would find but a limited audience, Leland noted in the preface: "There are few indeed who will care whether there is a veritable Gospel of the Witches, apparently of extreme antiquity embodying the belief in a strange counter-religion which has held its own from prehistoric time to the present day." And nearly seventy-five years would pass before the lore Leland regarded "as something to say the least, remarkable" would begin to receive the attention and appreciation it deserves.

Among the conjurations, spells and invocations of the *Vangelo* we find the allegorical tale of Aradia, born of the mating between the Lady of Darkness (Diana) and the Lord of Light (Lucifer), destined to teach the secret art of witchcraft to the children of Earth. Upon those Aradia favored were bestowed certain symbolic gifts:

To know success in love.

To bless or curse with power friends and enemies.

To converse with spirits.

To find hidden treasures in ancient ruins.

To conjure the spirits of priests who died leaving treasures.

To understand the voice of the wind.

To change water into wine.

To divine with cards.

To know the secrets of the hand.

To cure diseases.

To make those who are ugly, beautiful.

To tame wild beasts.

The MOON Calendar

is divided into zodiac signs rather than the more familiar Gregorian calendar.

2007

2008

Bear in mind that new projects should be initiated when the Moon is waxing (from dark to full); when the Moon is on the wane (from full to dark), it is a time for storing energy and the wise person waits.

Please note that Moons are listed by day of entry into each sign. Quarters are marked, but as rising and setting times vary from one region to another, it is advisable to check your local newspaper, library or planetarium.

The Moon's Place is computed for Eastern Standard Time.

The Magic of Sapphires

SAPPHIRES ARE cherished by mystics in every spiritual tradition as attractions of divine favor. Only the diamond rivals this lovely gem in popularity and durability. The sapphire is a valuable corundum crystal, usually a deep royal blue or sky blue. Opaque or clear, the distinctive blue derives from two mineral compounds, titanium and iron. Sapphires can also be pink, yellow or green if other minerals occur. Some of the most impressive sapphires are mined in Sri Lanka. Buddhists wear them to encourage devotion and speed up the process of enlightenment. Hindus place sapphires in gemstone tablets used as astrological charms. The sapphire is credited with bringing health, strength, energy and powerful friends. It also will banish evil spells, envy and protect from imprisonment.

In the mystical Cabbala the word *sephira* on the tree of life is a translation from the Hebrew of sapphire. The ten *sephiroth* are precious sapphires, jewels for following the path to universal knowledge. The legendary and elusive philosopher's stone, which grants wealth, wisdom and prophecy, was thought to be a sapphire.

In Germany sapphire legends relate to victory. The gems carry good luck from owner to owner. Historical accounts tell of the sapphire's ability to cure depression, fevers, ulcers, relieve boils and the plague as well as strengthen the eyes.

Star sapphires have rutiles or inclusions in the stone that appear like asterisks. In such gems three light bars cross to form six rays. The message conveyed is that faith, hope and a destiny or mission come with the stone. The Star of India is the most famous star sapphire. People believe that a benevolent spirit is entrapped, somewhat like a genie, within the stone.

The powerful and magical sapphire is a venerable talisman for all those who seek truth and uphold high ideals.

– GRANIA LING

aries
March 20 – April 19
Cardinal Sign of Fire △ Ruled by Mars ♂

S	M	T	W	T	F	S
		MAR. 20 2007 VERNAL EQUINOX Aries	21 Bless seeds Taurus	22	23 Gemini	24 Call a friend
25 Cancer	26 Joseph Campbell born, 1904	27 Be cautious Leo	28	29 Shake the hand of a child	30 Have dinner with a loved one Virgo	31
APRIL 1 Daylight Savings Time begins at 2 a.m.	2 Seed Moon Libra	3 Knot red thread for power	4 Exercise compassion Scorpio	5	6 Hold your temper	7 Sagittarius
8	9 Know your enemies Capricorn	10	11 Avoid a fool Aquarius	12	13 Stay indoors	14 Honor your mother Pisces
15 Leonardo DaVinci born, 1452	16 Tonight brings impor- tant dreams Aries	17	18 Plant seeds indoors Taurus	19		

KITCHEN MAGIC

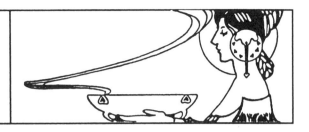

SEAFOOD IS TOUCHED with magic in Fiji, treated as treasure from a sacred source. This flavorful bouillabaisse, star of Sunday feasts, is a recipe that my father and I created over the years of my growing up in Fiji. My father was a marine engineer and on their days off the local Fijians, Indians and expatriates brought him their disabled engines. Most people had little money and bartered – gunny sacks of papayas, coconuts, cassava, taro, deep-sea fish, lobsters, rock crabs, blue prawns. The seafood went into the bouillabaisse prepared with a large stainless steel brazier, the fruit was passed around for dessert. Before we tasted a mouthful of food, we raised our coconut-shell bowls holding kava, brewed from the roots of a local plant. The toast was silent, but everyone at the table held the same thought – to salute the sea and thank our watery mother for her eternal nourishment.

FIJI BOUILLABAISSE
Polynesian Fish Stew

1 yellow onion, chopped
1/4 cup olive oil
2 tablespoons each grated ginger
   and chopped garlic
3 roma tomatoes, chopped
1 fennel bulb, sliced
1 pound mussels, cleaned well
1/4 pound halibut or mahi-mahi
1/4 pound medium prawns,
   shelled and deveined, or 1 lobster,
   cut into pieces
Salt and pepper
1 teaspoon saffron
4 mint leaves, crushed

   In a stainless steel pan sauté onions in oil until light brown. Add ginger and garlic and sauté for about 1 minute. Add tomatoes and fennel and sauté for 5 minutes. Put in seafood and sauté for three minutes longer. Season with salt and pepper. Add 5 cups water and saffron and simmer the bouillabaisse over low heat for about 30 minutes. Add mint and correct the seasoning. Serve with garlic bread. Serves 4-6.

                – SUNITA DUTT

taurus
April 20 – May 20
Fixed Sign of Earth ♉ Ruled by Venus ♀

S	M	T	W	T	F	S
					APRIL 20 Gemini	21
22 Cancer	23 Gather pebbles	24 🌓 Leo	25 Ella Fitzgerald born, 1918	26 Plan your garden Virgo	27 Purchase a token of love	28
29 Libra	30 Roodmas Eve	MAY 1 BELTANE ✠ Dance the Maypole	2 (Hare Moon) Scorpio	3 Gaze at the moon	4 Sagittarius	5 Travel safely
6 Orson Welles born, 1915 Capricorn	7	8 WHITE LOTUS DAY Aquarius	9 Sing a song to Isis	10 🌗	11 Brew a tea for peace Pisces	12 Gift the trees with water
13 Aries	14 Cleanse your household	15 Embrace your inner strength Taurus	16 🌑	17 Whistle a tune Gemini	18 Cast a love spell	19 Good planting day Cancer
20						

The Celestial Sari

LONG AGO IN THE Indian sub-continent, from India to Nepal, Pakistan, Sri Lanka and even Bangladesh, the cosmos was believed to be one sacred length of fabric. Intricate woven designs symbolized life itself. The patterns of warp and weft revealed humanity's joys, heartaches, dreams and illusions of life. The various cultural influences were expressed in vivid textile designs as early as 3500 BCE. Muslins, silks, linens, brocades, chiffons and cottons combined in dramatic, imaginative ways. Eventually the precious cloths came to be coveted the world over. The Vedas, Hindu scriptures at least five thousand years old, mentioned sacred weaving. Unstitched fabric was cherished because of its purity, untainted by needles made of bone. Long ago, the mists of time cloud exactly when, the beautiful lengths of weaving began to be worn at *pujas*, or sacred ceremonies. Eighteenth-century icons survive showing goddesses and gods in graceful fabric draperies. Eventually the lengths of cloth were used as everyday wear.

The draped clothes worn by men, drawn through the legs and secured at the waist, are known as *dhotis*. In the West we are more familiar with the women's garb, the sari. The word derives from the Sanskrit word *sati*, meaning strip of cloth. Everything about the lovely garments carries subtle messages. Today a sari can indicate the region of residence, origin and social status of the wearer at a glance. The style in which the fabric is draped or tied as well as the color and type of material reveals much to the trained eye – evoking Scottish plaids created to identify kinsmen, friends or foes.

Saris require nine yards of length by four feet of width for an elaborate drapery, although some styles require much less. They are elegant, comfortable garments, the drapery flattering to all figures. For ceremonial wear, for a party or just for fashion pleasure, you might enjoy shopping for a length of beautiful fabric and creating your own sari art.

– MARINA BYRONY

gemini

May 21 – June 20

Mutable Sign of Air △ Ruled by Mercury ☿

S	M	T	W	T	F	S
	MAY 21 Leo	22 Have patience	23 Virgo	24 Plan a vacation	25 Ralph Waldo Emerson born, 1803	26 Wish upon a cloud Libra
27 Whisper into the wind	28	29 OAK APPLE DAY Scorpio	30 Make a wish upon the moon	31 Dyad Moon Sagittarius	JUNE 1 Watch the moon rise	2 Count the birds
3 Capricorn	4 Bring peace to the angry	5 Night of the Watchers Aquarius	6 Don't judge friends	7 Avoid delay Pisces	8	9 Johnny Depp born, 1963 Aries
10 Find a shooting star	11 Weed the garden Taurus	12	13 Take solace in shadows Gemini	14	15 Summon a love	16 Spend today with your familiar Cancer
17 Igor Stravinsky born, 1882	18 Light a candle for strength Leo	19	20 Fairy's Day Virgo			

CLASSICAL MOONS

Artemis. Greek goddess of wild nature, associated with the Moon as her twin brother, Apollo, is with the Sun.

Cynthia. A name for the Moon derived from Mount Cynthus on the Greek island of Delos where Leto gave birth to Artemis and Apollo.

Diana. An Italian wood deity identified with the Greek Artemis and, like her, symbolized the Moon.

Hecate. A primitive Greek goddess of three realms – heaven, earth, and sea. The Moon before rising, after setting, and for the three nights when it is lost from sight belong to Hecate.

Luna. A Roman epithet for the Moon goddess depicted as winged and driving a chariot drawn by two white horses.

Phoebe. When a bright Moon shines high in the sky, Artemis is called Phoebe as her twin Apollo becomes Phoebus in bright aspect.

Selene. The Moon goddess in the Greek legend who fell in love with the sleeping shepherd boy Endymion.

Trivia. The triple-form of Hecate and the Moon made the location where three roads met sacred – *tri*, three and *via*, road. The Romans knew Hecate as Trivia, goddess of witchcraft.

cancer

June 21 – July 22

Cardinal Sign of Water ▽ Ruled by Moon ☽

S	M	T	W	T	F	S
				June 21 SUMMER SOLSTICE ☼	22 Libra	23 *Gather berries*
24 *Gather solar herbs*	25 *See a frog and know truth* Scorpio	26	27 *Take heed* Sagittarius	28 *Honesty comes easily*	29 *Patience brings success*	30 Mead Moon Capricorn
July 1	2 *Gather seashells* Aquarius	3 *Reveal a deception*	4 *Think about yesterday* Pisces	5	6 *Rescue a broken heart* Aries	7
8 *Have tea with a friend*	9 Taurus	10 *Hold fast to your principles*	11 *Weed your garden* Gemini	12 *Consult the tarot*	13 *John Dee born, 1527* Cancer	14
15 *Laughter quenches anger* Leo	16 *Have faith*	17 *False trials* Virgo	18 *Wish upon still waters*	19 *Lizzie Borden born, 1860*	20 *Dry your tears* Libra	21 *A tempest brews*
22						

The Frog and the Ox

Aesop's Fables   Illustrated by Arthur Rackham

"Oh, Father," said a little frog sitting by the side of a pool. "I have seen such a terrible monster! It was big as a mountain with horns on its head and a long tail and it had hoofs divided in two."

"Tush, child," said the old Frog, "that was only Farmer White's Ox. It isn't so big either; he may be a little bit taller than I, but I could easily make myself quite as broad." So he blew himself out and blew himself out. "Was he that big?" the father asked.

"Oh, much bigger than that," said the young Frog.

Again the old one blew himself out, and asked the young one if the Ox was that big.

"Bigger, Father, bigger," was the reply.

So the Frog took a deep breath, and blew and blew and blew, and swelled and swelled and swelled. Then he said, "I'm sure the Ox is not as big as..." But at this moment he burst.

MORAL: Self-conceit may lead to self-destruction.

leo

July 23 – August 22

Fixed Sign of Fire △ Ruled by Sun ☉

LEO

S	M	T	W	T	F	S
	July 23 *Play music to the stars* Scorpio	24 *Amelia Earhart born, 1898*	25 Sagittarius	26 *Beware the storm*	27 *Set goals* Capricorn	28
29 (Wort Moon) Aquarius	30 *Bake bread*	31 *Eve of Lughnassad*	August 1 LAMMAS ♑ Pisces	2 *Enjoy a feast*	3 *Soften the passion* Aries	4 *Wear amber for luck*
5 Taurus	6 *Contemplate your health*	7 Gemini	8 *Dispel fear*	9 *Take your fill* Cancer	10 *Cat familiars need attention*	11 *The sun rules this day* Leo
12	13 DIANA'S DAY Virgo	14	15 *Travel light*	16 *Give laughter* Libra	17 *Mae West born, 1892*	18 *Carry gold for health*
19 *Don't fret, clouds move on* Scorpio	20	21 Sagittarius	22 *Remember a love*			

The Queen Bee

Arthur Rackham

THREE PRINCES once set off in search of adventure. The two elder brothers mocked the youngest, whom they called Blockhead, for his nature was simple. As they traveled, they came across an anthill. The elder brothers wanted to destroy it, but Blockhead made them leave the ants alone. Then they saw some ducks swimming, and wanted to roast them, but Blockhead made them leave them alone. When they spied a beehive, they wanted to light a fire so that they could take the honey, but Blockhead made them leave the creatures in peace.

Finally the three came to an enchanted castle. A little man told them that three princesses lay asleep within. If the brothers could do three tasks, they would win the princesses. If not, they would be turned to stone.

The first task was to gather a thousand pearls that lay hidden in the moss of the forest. The first two brothers failed, and were turned to stone. But when Blockhead tried, the ants he had saved brought the pearls to him. Then he had to get the key to the princesses' room. The key lay at the bottom of a lake, and Blockhead despaired until the ducks he had saved got the key for him. For his final task, Blockhead had to determine which of the princesses was youngest and sweetest. They all looked the same. The only difference was this: at their last meal, the youngest had eaten honey, while the others had eaten some sugar and some syrup. The queen of the bees Blockhead had saved flew into the room and alighted on the lips of the youngest and sweetest princess, for she could still taste the bit of honey. When the prince awoke her, his brothers revived. Blockhead married the youngest and sweetest. Never again did his elder brothers make sport of him.

– From The Brothers Grimm

38

virgo

August 23 – September 22

Mutable Sign of Earth ▽ Ruled by Mercury ☿

S	M	T	W	T	F	S
				Aug. 23 *Barbara Eden born, 1934* Capricorn	24	25 *Footprints in the sand*
26 Aquarius	27 *Full Moon total lunar eclipse* ⇨	28 Barley Moon Pisces	29 *Reflect on lessons learned*	30 Aries	31	Sept. 1 *Bake a pie with love* Taurus
2 *Enjoy friends and family*	3 Gemini	4 *Conversation turns serious*	5 *Gather beach sand for divining* Cancer	6	7 *Lighten the disposition* Leo	8 *Richard the Lion-Hearted born, 1157*
9 *Hold tight to a dream*	10 *New Moon partial solar eclipse* ⇨ Virgo	11	12 Libra	13 *Bless a home*	14	15 *Develop secret talents* Scorpio
16 *Honor your elders*	17 *Wash with sea water*	18 Sagittarius	19	20 *Heed the tree's words of wisdom* Capricorn	21	22 *Eat cookies* Aquarius

The wizard escapes

From Olaus Magnus' Historia de gentibus septentrionalibus, *Rome, 1555*

THERE WAS A WIZARD held in prison by a Pasha. The Pasha brought him out to do tricks in front of guests. Bring a bowl of water, said the wizard. Now, this water is the sea. And what port shall I show you on the sea? Show a port on the island of Malta, they said. And there it was. Houses and churches and a steamer ready to sail. Now would you like to see me step aboard that steamer? And the Pasha laughed, Go ahead! So the wizard put his foot in the bowl of water and stepped on board the steamer and went to America! What do you think of that!

– The Albanian Virgin, ALICE MUNRO

libra

September 23 – October 23

Cardinal Sign of Air ♎ Ruled by Venus ♀

LIBRA

S	M	T	W	T	F	S
SEPT. 23 FALL EQUINOX ☋	24 Don't be fooled Pisces	25 Watch the waves	26 (Blood Moon) Aries	27	28 Encourage stability in a loved one Taurus	29
30 Gemini	OCT. 1	2 See with the jackal's eyes Cancer	3	4 Make an herbal wreath	5 Leo	6 Gather acorns for spells
7 Obstacles bring options Virgo	8	9 Distinction brings pain Libra	10 Chant for peace	11	12 You find a guide Scorpio	13 Gather fallen leaves
14 Sagittarius	15 Find comfort in dreams	16 Be playful	17	18 Nicholas Culpeper born, 1616 Capricorn	19 Aquarius	20 Use your creativity
21	22 Pisces	23				

TAROT'S DEATH

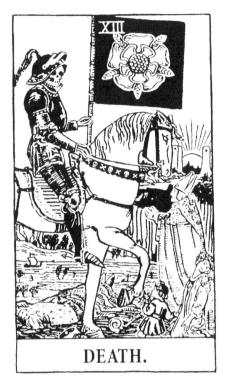

DEATH.

Rider-Waite-Smith deck

Number 13 of the Major Arcana may be the most misunderstood card of the Tarot deck. Rarely does it presage literal physical death. The embedded meaning portrays symbolic death – a change or transformation.

A skeleton rides a white horse, and beneath its hooves lie figures of all ranks – kings, bishops, villagers. But the black banner holds a white flower, an indication of a garden, of rebirth. When the card appears in your reading, it may be a challenge to embrace change in aspects of your life where you need to clean out the old and make way for the new. The time is now to face decisions you may have been reluctant to address; the card alerts the seeker against procrastination. However, just drawing the card indicates a readiness for change, even though the seeker may not consciously be aware of it. The Death card asks you to let go, move on, and rejoice in the creativity of change, the universal constant.

scorpio
October 24 – November 21
Fixed Sign of Water ▽ Ruled by Pluto ♀

S	M	T	W	T	F	S
			Oct. 24 *Burn patchouli incense* Aries	25 *Pablo Picasso born, 1881*	26 Snow Moon	27 *Beckon a spirit*
28 *Daylight Savings Time ends at 2 a.m.* Gemini	29 *Hide the salt*	30 *Stir a cauldron 3 times 3* Cancer	31 *Eve of Hallowmas*	Nov. 1 Leo	2 *Rest*	3 *Admire ancestors' photos* Virgo
4 *Honor your siblings*	5 *Dispel evil*	6 *Gift garlic* Libra	7 *There was but one of you*	8 *Befriend a spirit* Scorpio	9	10 *Study ancient lore*
11 *Contemplate and reflect* Sagittarius	12	13 *Draw on your passions* Capricorn	14 *Gather kindling*	15	16 HECATE NIGHT Aquarius	17
18 *Alan Shepard born, 1923* Pisces	19	20 *Beware of fires* Aries	21 *Focus inward*			

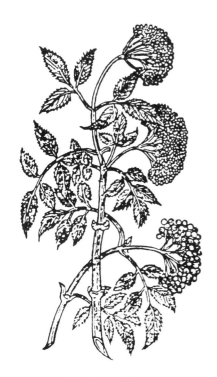

Sambucas Nigra

Elder

November 25 to December 22

DIANA OF EPHESUS was originally worshipped in the form of a date palm, and the elder tree of Northern Europe once had a similar resident deity whose magical significance has lasted through the centuries. Scandinavian legends tell of the Elder Mother who watches for any injury to the tree. If even a sprig is cut without first asking permission of the Elder Mother, whatever purpose the sprig is cut for will end in misfortune.

Once permission has been asked and a twig of the elder secured, it will banish evil spirits and may be hung or worn as an amulet. Elder flowers, dried while the moon waxes from dark to full, are a potent love charm. The berries gathered at summer solstice afford protection from all unexpected dangers, including accidents and lightning strikes.

Beyond its subtle gifts, the elder offers healing for a variety of ailments. Its leaves are an effective insect repellent; its close-grained wood finds favor with carpenters; its berries provide a deep purple dye as well as culinary treats and the renowned elderberry wine.

Reverence for the Elder Mother challenged the early Christian church fathers and soon missionary priests redefined the tree goddess as a wicked witch more to be feared than adored. Moreover, Judas, betrayer of Christ, hanged himself on an elder tree, and Christ was crucified on a cross of elder. To place a baby in an elder cradle invited an evil spirit to come and snuff out its life. The tree constituted so serious a threat that England's King Edgar in the tenth century issued a warning against "those vain practices which are carried on with Elders."

Folklore passed down to us today reflects these ambivalent attitudes, for elder is more often considered evil than good. Only in Denmark has the Elder Mother, *Hylde-Moer,* retained her sacred nature. Hans Christian Andersen's tale of the Elder Mother who becomes a beautiful maiden named Memory captures the spirit of the most ancient lore.

– FROM *Celtic Tree Magic*
BY ELIZABETH PEPPER

sagittarius

November 22 – December 21

Mutable Sign of Fire △ Ruled by Jupiter ♃

S	M	T	W	T	F	S
				Nov. 22 Taurus	23 Boris Karloff born, 1887	24 Oak Moon Gemini
25	26 Scry to reveal secrets Cancer	27	28 Leo	29	30	Dec. 1 ◑ Virgo
2	3 Greet Jack Frost Libra	4 Guard the threshold	5 Walt Disney born, 1901 Scorpio	6	7 Bitterness is overcome	8 Perform a divination Sagittarius
9 ●	10 Gather evergreens and holly	11 Capricorn	12 Make wassail	13 Light candles! Aquarius	14 Nostradamus born, 1503	15 Pisces
16 Fairy Queen Eve	17 ◐ Aries	18 Unlock the mind's door	19 Bake sweets Taurus	20	21 Light the Yule log Gemini	

Everything suddenly makes sense

Only reincarnation offers a plausible explanation for the seeming inequities of our physical world; only reincarnation gives us hope that we do have certain controls over an otherwise prearranged destiny: our behavior, our attitudes, our way of life… and after-life. Nothing stirs up more questions than the system of rebirth cycles in human existence. Those who will accept the system as natural and all-pervasive will find their lives falling into place differently than before. Everything moves as it ought to – even if some experiences are not pleasant – and there is frustration mixed in with success and joy.

– Life Beyond Life, HANS HOLZER

capricorn
December 22 – January 19
Cardinal Sign of Earth ▽ Ruled by Saturn ♄

S	M	T	W	T	F	S
						Dec. **22** WINTER SOLSTICE ☉
23 Wolf Moon ○ Cancer	**24** Burn candles of gold	**25** Hail the Newborn Sun	**26** Leo	**27** Eat walnuts for health	**28** Virgo	**29** Lovingly train your pet
30	**31** ◐ Libra	Jan. **1**	**2** Offer support Scorpio	**3**	**4** Soft fires offer romance Sagittarius	**5**
6 Alan Watts born, 1915	**7** Prepare goals for coming year Capricorn	**8** ●	**9** JANUS DAY Aquarius	**10** Exercise your body and mind	**11**	**12** Play games Pisces
13 Take a deep breath	**14**	**15** ◑ Aries	**16** Avoid being stubborn Taurus	**17** Strengthen your spirit	**18** Move with grace Gemini	**19** Edgar Allan Poe born, 1809

Martines de Pasqually

"This extraordinary man is the only living man I have known whom I have not fathomed."

SO WROTE Louis-Claude de Saint-Martin, a profound mystic and philosopher in his own right. As a youth he had known Martines de Pasqually well. He was an early initiate into Pasqually's Order of the Elect Cohens (Ordre des Élus Coëns), and he knew its doctrines and rituals well. After Pasqually's death, Saint-Martin took a different esoteric path, but he always praised the knowledge and power of his first master.

In 1774 Martines de Pasqually died unexpectedly, only some twenty years after he had formed the first temples, or lodges, of his order in several French cities. He had not transmitted all his doctrines and practices of his order by the time of his death, and the order itself only lasted a few decades longer. Yet some of his manuscripts and letters to his initiates have survived. None of them have been translated from the French into English. From them we can learn much about his doctrines and also something about the rituals of his order.

Pasqually always claimed that what he transmitted was a secret tradition handed down by his family in Spain, which he had learned directly from his father. Though Pasqually himself was a Roman Catholic, some of his remote Spanish ancestors were converted Jews. So it is not surprising that Pasqually's esoteric work has strong affinities with Jewish mysticism in general and with the kabbalah of Isaac Luria in particular. Pasqually offered to his initiates a variety of Jewish-Christian gnosis – transcendent knowledge that envisioned overcoming the barriers that presently separate fallen humankind and all creation from the luminous realms of spirits, angels and God. The philosopher also offered his adherents a set of rituals for them to work in company with these luminous spirits, angels, and even God. He believed that such observances might lead to the visible manifestation of these higher beings within the room of the temple. Saint-Martin says that he witnessed such manifestations more than once.

But these manifestations were not the ultimate aim of the rituals. That was nothing less than the eventual reintegration of all created beings into an unbroken whole, as before Adam's fall. Pasqually's best-known writing is "A Treatise on the Reintegration of Created Beings in their Original Divine Properties, Virtues and Powers." Due to their high aims and impressive results, Pasqually's doctrines and practices deserve the attention of esotericists even today.

The best accounts of Martines de Pasqually in English are found in the excellent *Dictionary of Gnosis and Western Esotericism*, edited by Wouter J. Hanegraaff and others, 2 vols. (Leiden: Brill, 2005). See the substantial articles on "Élus Coëns," on "Martinism: First Period," and on "Pasqually, Martines de.")

– ROBERT MATHIESEN

aquarius

January 20 – February 18

Fixed Sign of Air ♎ Ruled by Uranus ♅

S	M	T	W	T	F	S
Jan. 20 Cancer	21	22 Storm Moon Leo	23 *The point of stability*	24 *Read a book* Virgo	25 *Virginia Woolf, born, 1882*	26
27 *Feed the birds* Libra	28 *Polish silver and shine mirrors*	29 *Trim a broom* Scorpio	30	31	Feb. 1 *Write a poem* Sagittarius	2 CANDLE-MAS
3 Capricorn	4 *Remember a childhood tale*	5 *New Moon partial solar eclipse* ⇨	6 **Year of the Rat** Aquarius	7	8 *Wear something indigo* Pisces	9 *Decorate a room in the home*
10 Aries	11	12 *Refresh indoor plants* Taurus	13	14 *Enjoy music* Gemini	15 LUPER-CALIA	16 *Play a concert in your mind* Cancer
17	18 *Ramakrishna born, 1836* Leo					

Charms for Neptune's Favors

THE URGE TO GIVE one's self up to the wonders of water has long been a source of joy. A cool dip on a hot summer day is a childhood memory cherished by many, and most of us still enjoy a day at the beach. Just a breeze from sea, river or lake offers refreshment. Evidence exists that contact with the crystals in salt water as well as negative ions generated by waterfalls have the ability to heal the mind as well as the body.

Once our feet leave the shore we are forever visitors in another realm, and there is another side to our pleasure. A deadly rip current, high winds or attack from Jaws can quickly turn the idyllic experience into a nightmare.

Early mythology always recognized the sea as a living, conscious entity. Prayers to Neptune for safe passage as well as charms against sea serpents have been recorded for thousands of years. Sailors often carried a seashell from their home ports to assure a safe return.

For swimming or boating, emulate the time-honored sailors by making personal shell charms:

When the Moon is new in a water sign, collect or purchase a shell pleasing to you. Find one with a natural hole or drill one. String the shell on a cord and reverently chant the name of Neptune or another favored water deity. Bury the shell in a dish of sea salt to be charged with protective forces until the Full Moon rises, then remove the charm. Toss the salt into the water you are about to enter as an offering and hold the shell aloft in the moonlight. The shell charm will be ready to wear as you enter the water.

Surfers at Florida's Sebastian Inlet usually possess a special charm. The waves at the inlet are notoriously shark infested. A shark's tooth added to a choker of puka shells is worn as a warning. The idea is that the sharks will stay away, sensing what happened to the last one who bothered the surfer. Puka shells are the small tops of the Pacific Island conus shell. They have a natural hole and were collected in Hawaii to be worn by island queens and princesses as adornments and talismans. Pisces Elizabeth Taylor was given puka shells as a ceremonial gift from the sea during a 1974 visit to Hawaii. She wore them publicly often. With or without a shark's-tooth pendant, a puka choker is a beautiful and powerful talisman to wear against the perils of the briny deep.

– ESTHER ELAYNE

pisces
February 19 – March 20
Mutable Sign of Water ▽ Ruled by Neptune ♆

S	M	T	W	T	F	S
		Feb. 19 Full Moon total lunar eclipse ⇨	20 Chaste Moon Virgo	21	22 Sample confections	23 Libra
24 Steve Jobs born, 1955	25	26 Scorpio	27 Send a letter	28 Sagittarius	March 1 Avoid idle conversation	2 Capricorn
3	4 Assess your spiritual growth Aquarius	5	6 Clean out closets Pisces	7	8 Enjoy solitude	9 Aries
10 Make a wish	11 Visit an old home Taurus	12	13 Gemini	14	15 Hug a dear one Cancer	16 Make a pillow
17 Leo	18 Edgar Cayce born, 1877	19 Use vervain in a spell Virgo	20 Spot a rabbit			

Water, Water, Everywhere

At all times and in all places, writers have paid tribute to our Great Salty Mother and her numerous progeny.

I would be a mermaid fair;
I would sing to myself the
  whole of the day;
With a comb of pearl I would
  comb my hair;
And still as I comb I would
  sing and say,
"Who is it loves me?
  who loves not me?"

– Alfred Lord Tennyson

We call upon the waters that rim the earth, horizon to horizon, that flow in our rivers and streams, that fall upon our gardens and fields, and we ask that they teach us and show us the way.

– Chinook blessing

You could not step twice into the same river, for other waters are ever flowing on to you.

–Heraclitus of Ephesus

The cure for anything is salt water – sweat, tears, or the sea.

– Isak Dinesen

Water is the driver of Nature.

– Leonardo DaVinci

I am sure it is a great mistake always to know enough to go in when it rains. One may keep snug and dry by such knowledge, but one misses a world of loveliness.

– Adeline Knapp

Water flows humbly to the lowest level. Nothing is weaker than water, yet for overcoming what is hard and strong, Nothing surpasses it.

– Lao Tzu

For whatever we lose
(like a you or a me),
It's always our self
we find in the sea.

– e. e. cummings

It is an important and popular fact that things are not always what they seem. For instance, on the planet Earth, man had always assumed that he was more intelligent than dolphins because he had achieved so much – the wheel, New York, wars and so on – whilst all the dolphins had ever done was muck about in the water having a good time. But conversely, the dolphins had always believed that they were far more intelligent than man – for precisely the same reasons.

– Douglas Adams

Window on the Weather

Our daily weather is controlled by large-scale natural cycles that bring the earth's climate into long-term balances. Forces of almost unimaginable power and elegance redirect excesses of heat and cold in an efficient manner. Warmth is carried north from the tropics replacing cold that naturally flows south, both in rhythmic patterns. Our planet's surface is characterized by variations of substances and color. Oceans, ice, mountains and plains all accept the sun's energy at different rates. Warmth is immediately deflected back into space by light-colored surfaces such as ice and snow, while dark-colored surfaces such as earth and rock accept the sun's radiation more readily. These imbalances of earth's heat budget are constantly brought into natural distributions by the weather that we all experience. Climate patterns are harmonious, yet defined by their certitude, little influenced in their scope by manmade influence.

– Tom C. Lang

SPRING

MARCH 2007. The lingering effects of the El Niño event that began last summer will bring an increased frequency of strong thunderstorms and in general an early start to the severe weather season in the South. With the weak nature of this year's El Niño occurrence and a decreased amount of energy from the sun, temperatures will remain cold enough in the Northeast, Rocky Mountain States and the Sierra Nevada of California to bring late winter snowfall. March storms will trend stronger with abundant moisture. Storms traversing the country will leave a widespread blanket of snow. Only the Deep South and Florida will experience above-normal temperatures. There rough weather is punctuated by hail and high winds with the possibility of wet snow in the Southern Appalachians.

APRIL 2007. The Pacific Ocean is the source of several phenomena that combine with other factors to govern the strength and path of storms and regulate the flow of heat around the globe. The best-known examples of these catalysts are El Niño and La Niña, which offer considerable opposing impacts. El Niños generally bring wet and sometimes cold patterns to the Northern Hemisphere, while La Niñas generally produce warm and dry conditions. A third mode, most recently understood, is called "La Nada," characterized by a reversion to the most recent ebbing El Niño or La Niña event. This occurrence will produce a continuation of the weather patterns chronicled in March, with late-season snows continuing, especially at higher elevations in the East, West and a quickening pace of severe weather outbreaks in the Southeast, particularly in Georgia, Alabama and the Southern Plains. Southern California storms bring mud slides.

MAY 2007. May is generally the peak of the tornado season nationwide, both with respect to geographic distribution and intensity. While it was once believed that Texas and Oklahoma experienced the strongest tornadoes, Alabama is now considered the focal point of these devastating storms. This is probably due to the extreme warmth associated with the Gulf of Mexico waters that feed into the Southeast. The threat is particularly urgent this year.

In the spring, the jet stream is usually aligned in the lower Ohio Valley and Great Plains, where the greatest number of tornadoes will occur this year. Rainfall will again be above normal this month in the Northeast, where several storms of long duration will bring flooding. Late season rains will fill reservoirs in the west. The snowmelt in the Rockies will be slowed by late season cold weather.

SUMMER

JUNE 2007. With wind fields and moisture focused along the U.S./Canadian border, much of the Northeast, Ohio Valley and Great Lake States will again experience above-normal rainfall. Disturbances will probably move quickly within this airflow, yet rainfall can be intense, falling within a short time frame of several hours. Embedded within these fast-moving systems will be thunderstorms, some with squalls of wind and rain. In the Southwest, weather systems will move much more slowly. Covering sea breezes will have various impacts in Florida. On the Florida East Coast, showers will generally occur in the morning, while late afternoon thunderstorms can be intense on the Florida West Coast from Tampa to Naples during the late afternoon. An early hurricane season will bring rainfall along the Continental Divide in the West, with beautiful weather along the West Coast and Pacific Northwest.

JULY 2007. The pace of weather changes will remain steady in the North, with frequent bouts of showers and thunderstorms. Squall lines are created ahead of cold fronts by a process called a gravity wave. Energy is sent forth from an advancing cold front, producing long clusters of thunderstorms. They generally move very quickly and while tornadoes are infrequent with these severe weather outbreaks, strong, damaging winds can occur. These will be frequent this summer, with corresponding rapid changes in temperature from day to day. Steady southeast winds will bring late afternoon showers often in Atlanta, northward to the Southern Appalachians. Flash flooding can occur there. Dry weather with near record heat is likely in the Great Plains, while the West enjoys fine midsummer weather.

AUGUST 2007. Common weather news terms generated by the media may be confusing. For example, a tornado or severe thunderstorm "watch" is issued when conditions are favorable for the formation of those storms. "Warnings" of those systems arise when either is actually pending. "Severe thunderstorms" are defined by winds exceeding 59 miles per hour, large hail and frequent and dangerous cloud-to-ground lightning.

These storms will be most common this year in the Northern Plains, Great Lakes States and through mid-month in the Northeast. Intense heat will linger in the nation's heartland, with thunderstorms frequently occurring in Florida as the Atlantic hurricane season begins.

AUTUMN

SEPTEMBER 2007. An El Niño event has a profound effect on the hurricane season in both the Atlantic and Pacific Oceans. Activity is profound in the Pacific Ocean, though these storms generally have little impact on land masses, except occasionally on the West Coast of Mexico. Atlantic activity is often quelled. This will probably be the course of events this year, though a major hurricane can still impact the East Coast or Gulf Coast. The weather turns quiet elsewhere. The rainy weather pattern will be quelled in the Northeast as cool air infiltrates the region. Mountainous rainfall is more frequent in the West as Pacific moisture moves north. Mid-continent heat is slow to ease with frequent daily highs in the 80s and 90s.

OCTOBER 2007. Hurricane formation is generally confined to the Caribbean and Eastern Atlantic Basin. Water temperatures cool to levels below those that support this activity elsewhere. Therefore tropical storms and hurricanes tend to be weaker and the threat to the East Coast diminishes. October is also the driest time of the year. Available tropical moisture, critical for northern storm formation, is pushed south by the jet stream's return south from Canada. Snowfall begins in the highest peaks of the Northern Rockies. Leaves begin their annual color change, the result of diminishing sunlight. Great ranges of daily temperatures are felt, especially at mid-continent with chilly mornings and mild afternoons. Rainfall is sparse in the East, while tornado formation is limited to the Southern Great Plains.

NOVEMBER 2007. As the influence of the Pacific Ocean oscillations shifts from an El Niño mode to La Niña, the effect on North America results in a change in the jet stream pattern. It dips in the West, bringing early season snow to the Rocky Mountains and Sierra Nevada of California. At first the influence in the East is more subtle; temperatures will trend above normal, especially in the Southeast where rainfall will be sparse. The Northeast and Mid Atlantic will experience relatively dry conditions as well, though a brief early season snowfall can occur there at month's end. The weather is especially dry across the Great Lakes. Lake effect snowfall is sparse as the ground remains bare. Much of the East will wait for the arrival of winter conditions.

WINTER

DECEMBER 2007. A subtle shift in various air flows will bring a gradual evolution to winter conditions in the Northeast. Limited incursions of chilly Canadian air will be positioned to interact with a series of weak disturbances carried northward by the jet stream. The position of the cold air in relation to these weak low pressure centers will bring a number of moderate snowfalls from the Ohio Valley to New England. A steady snowpack will deepen as the month progresses, cold air remains persistent.

The Southeast will remain warm and quite dry. Florida will be especially prone to wildfires. The Pacific Northwest will be unusually cold with snow falling close to Seattle and bring hazardous travel conditions to the highway on Route 5 through Washington and Oregon.

JANUARY 2008. The Northeast will be covered by a shallow layer of cold air early in the month that will contribute to the possibility of a serious ice storm. Many residents still remember a similar weather system that left many communities without power for two weeks. Precautions should therefore be taken. The Southeast will remain very dry and quite warm, with temperatures reaching the seventies several times from Georgia to Florida. Snow will fall on occasion from North Texas to the high plains. Ski conditions will be fine in the Rockies and California with some long-lasting snowfalls. Southern California will find windy and warm conditions with the fire danger quite high.

FEBRUARY 2008. A prolonged series of moderate snowfalls will blanket the Ohio Valley and Northeast this month. Snowfall totals will be well above normal, though temperatures will not be particularly cold. The snow cover should last into the early spring there. Wildfires linger in the Southeast, with very dry conditions persisting. Snowfall is also heavy in the Northern Plains with a blizzard possible in Minneapolis and Chicago at the end of the month. The Pacific Northwest is unusually dry and mild while the Rockies experience continuing winter storms.

The buzz on honeybees

BEES RELATE to humankind on both ends of the pain/pleasure continuum, from sting to honey. We forgive the bees their occasional hostility for providing us with honey, one of the most delicious of foods, a sticky substance that makes endorphins dance. We love honey on toast in the morning, Brits spread it on scones in the afternoon, Greeks enjoy flaky baklava as dessert. Fermented honey becomes mead, created before wine and the most ancient alcoholic drink, discovered in Scottish tombs from the Iron Age.

The world has more bees than you may imagine – twenty thousand species buzz around, although we take honey from only four types in the U.S., principally *Apis mellifera*. Honeybees long have played an important role in mythology and folklore almost everywhere. In the Near East and Aegean worlds, people believed that honeybees could travel to the underworld and buzz messages to the gods. The Minoan *tholos* tombs took the form of beehives; bees and honey were arranged in graves. Alexander the Great rests in a honey-filled coffin.

Perhaps this divinity connection accounted for bees' status as the "wisest of insects" in many cultures, credited with esoteric powers. The Pythian pre-Olympian priestess remained the "Delphic bee" long after Apollo had usurped her role as oracle, and the Homeric Hymn to Apollo acknowledges that the god's gift of prophecy derived

from three bee-maidens. Apollo's sister Artemis shared his bond with bees. In her later role as Diana of Ephesus, beehives symbolized the deity's fertility rites. Her cult was called the "hive," her priests and priestesses "worker bees." Demeter's priestesses were similarly termed, and their goddess was the "queen bee."

The Greeks offered libations of honey to their gods, and believed it to be the food of muses and poets. As for honey fermented into mead, in the classical Greek language "honey-intoxicated" was a pleasant term for drunk.

Bees lost none of their symbolic meaning with the rise of Christianity. Mary, like Demeter before her, was known as the "queen bee," Christ the

Dawnsio, dawnsio, little bees –
keep to your hives and do not roam.
– From a witch's blessing for honey

"honey." Christian tradition kept up the bees' connection to the underworld, too, calling them "little winged servants of God" and comparing their springtime emergence from hives to Christ's emergence from the tomb. New stories about bees also arose, such as the Welsh legend that they originated in Paradise, where they were white, and turned brown only after Adam and Eve ate the forbidden fruit.

Modern beliefs emphasize the bond between bees and beekeepers. Bees will not stay with a bad-tempered keeper. Bees must know everything that happens to the owner's family; births, illnesses, deaths. Some cultures go as far as including bees in weddings or funerals, tying red or black cloths to the top of hives and bringing sugary food to the bees while guests are feasting. Cornish tradition warns that you will get stung if you move a hive without telling the inhabitants. In many parts of the world a keeper's heir must inform the bees of the keeper's death by knocking three times on each hive with an iron key. If the bees buzz response, they are assuring their new owner that they will remain.

Bees also remain creatures of prophecy, but only single bees signify luck. Swarms of honeybees are ill omened and associated with bereavement. A honeybee landing on a hand means money coming in. A honeybee landing on a head indicates great future success. In Wales, a bee flying around a child's head foretells a happy life. A bee in the house assures good luck in Cornwall, as long as it is allowed to fly away or remain of its own will.

Nine thousand years of history and impressive powers indicate that the "wisest of insects" deserve respect. Little wonder that at one time you could only purchase bees with gold, and to gift a friend with a hive assured both honey and good luck.

– MOONDANCER

Sacred Wells

WATER IS the element that cleanses and purifies regardless of whether its form is liquid, ice, or steam. In ancient Britain places where water bubbled from the earth, such as underground streams, were regarded as miraculous and deemed sacred. Such a site was also considered to be a doorway to the Otherside – a place not a place, the boundary between dark and light, night and day, where one could converse with the dead or offer prayers to the gods.

In later times, when western Europe was being Christianized, the wells that had been dedicated to the old gods were now places for saints, although the worship styles remained unchanged. Wells ranging from a few stone markers to elaborate architecture became places of worship where pilgrims would come at certain times to drink the water, believing it to have healing properties. Sometimes the water from the well itself would be considered to be an aspect of the gods, so the drinker would be creating an inner sacred place, blending the spirit and the mundane. Others would leave coins or kiss the stones, even walking around the well a specified number of times to have wishes and prayers granted. Often a sacred tree would be found just near the well, frequently a hawthorn, hazel, rowan or yew. Pieces of cloth were tied to the branches, usually red to symbolize the Goddess. These trees were and still are called "clootie" trees, "clootie" being a Scottish term meaning "cloth."

The Chalice Well at Glastonbury, England, was the only well to provide water during the drought of 1921 and is still visited annually by thousands. In the gardens, one part of the well is protected from debris by a lid bearing the Vesica Piscis symbol – two conjoined circles, intersected by a line or "lance." The symbolism is sacred to many religions and recurs throughout the gardens. In China, drinking the water at the Pon Lai fountain is said to bless one with a thousand lives. For millennia water has been used for divining, and the springs at the temple of Demeter in Patras are specifically consulted for prophecy. And for water as the ultimate sacred healer, consider the Irish myth about the well of Airmed of Slane, where spells were sung into the depths. Then the dead killed in battle were placed into the waters and restored to life.

All over the world and in all times, wells and springs inspire similar beliefs about the ability of water to nourish both body and spirit.

– HELENA FIRTH

Merry Meetings

*A candle in the window, a fire on the hearth,
a conversation over tea…*

From time to time, *The Witches' Almanac* will offer interviews with noted members of the Craft community. The first such to grace our pages is the conversation below with the late Elizabeth Pepper:

Although one must admit that it's a subtle declaration, you have been referring to yourself obliquely as a "witch…from New England" on the title page of The Witches' Almanac *since its first publication in 1971. How did you come to define yourself as a witch or associate yourself with witchcraft?*

My parents and other members of our family practiced the Craft. All of them, in one way or another, taught me. The training was informal. You learned as you grew, selecting or rejecting whatever came into your scope. Speaking from my own experience, magic is something that is learned day by day in an indirect fashion. It can't be formally taught. And because there is no dogma, you evolve your own pattern.

That would place you in the somewhat controversial camp of hereditary, family, or traditional witches. Since authenticity is often called into question for those with this background, would you mind sharing some information regarding your lineage?

I was an only child; *the* only child on my mother's side of the family. I grew up in Providence, Rhode Island, on the East Side.

My father's family, the Peppers, came to this country in the sixteen-hundreds and there were English, Welsh, Scottish, Irish, Dutch and German surnames on the family tree. I gather that at least one member of each succeeding generation had an interest in or displayed an aptitude for witchcraft. The trait surfaced again and again.

My maternal grandmother was Spanish Basque. She met and married my grandfather, an Anglo-Irish sculptor whose specialty was gravestone angels, in London. They immigrated to America, settled in New England in 1887 and raised seven daughters and one son. I think it's unusual for an entire family to follow a single

occult path, but my mother's did. Six of my aunts lived within walking distance. Each one had a particular occult interest or talent. The mainspring of Craft traditions as I know them comes from them.

I think it is safe to say that growing up with an entire family that practices witchcraft is a rather unique experience that would place you in a minority among today's witches. Looking back on your childhood, what would you say are some of your greatest lessons or favorite memories?

It was fun. The Craft educates the heart and the spirit as well as the mind. Imagination is constantly encouraged and stimulated. I learned to recognize how commonplace things could be touched with magic. I have so many lovely memories — like being given my first kitten or watching the full moon rise for the first time. These were like sacred ceremonies, very solemn occasions.

Can you describe some of the magical work that you did with your family?

Dark of the Moon was the time for healings and forming rings of protection.

Tide Turnings, that's changing a run of bad luck by ritual, took place after the first quarter of the waxing moon. If someone had a near accident, a close call, and was haunted by it, the group would get together to remove the fright at full moon. Something was always happening—a disagreeable boss giving trouble, a love affair that wasn't working out—we'd concentrate to make it right, turning negatives to positives.

How old were you when you were allowed to participate in magical workings?

As soon as I could comprehend the nature of the problem to be solved or turned right, even in very simple terms, I joined my mind with the rest. Young children often bring a surprising amount of mental energy to the case at hand.

You say that the training was informal, unstructured, and that there is no dogma. If all of this is true, how does one come to define oneself as a witch? Is there an underlying moral or ethical code that you were taught to follow as a member of the Craft?

The first thing that comes to my mind is the deep and abiding love for animals. This is the one attribute every member of my family, all their friends, every single person we knew and associated with shared in common. I feel it is central to the recognition and practice of witchcraft. I realize that this is a sweeping statement, certain to provoke dissent. However, I'm absolutely convinced of its truth. Second is a sense of humor.

It's like a balance wheel. We should be serious in our work, or Craft undertakings, but not pious. "A witch isn't self-righteous" is the theme. Third – there is always a third, which is a tradition in itself – you can never refuse a cry for help. And when a gift is given or a favor done, the recipient is expected to pass the goodness along – not to necessarily repay the giver but to respond in a similar manner when the occasion arises. Other than that, I can only say that I think witchcraft is far more mysterious than anyone realizes.

You are far too engaged in the world around you to be accused of remaining aloof and unaware of the resurgence in witchcraft during the last five decades. How would you compare contemporary Craft to the Craft you were taught as a child?

Much of the lore and flavor is similar. Religion is far heavier a focus today than the Craft I grew up to know. That is not to say our work wasn't considered sacred, for it was very serious indeed. The structure of beliefs and ethical considerations were of an entirely different framework.

Elizabeth, you have always chosen to keep your personal life private. You've always denied having students,

stating simply that your teaching is done through your writing. You have no coven and you claim no initiates. You choose instead to be who you are and practice the Craft as a way of life, in the same manner that is was handed down to you. Why then, do you expose yourself to public scrutiny by publishing The Witches' Almanac*?*

I wanted to rid the Craft of its reputation of evil, horror, chicanery. I wanted to make it elegant; present its beauty, gentle nature, deep wisdom and simple good sense. I wanted to show that the Craft, like the Tao, is a way, an attitude toward living.

Finally, do you have any parting thoughts or words of advice?

Witchcraft fills a need for beauty, faith, romance, and a sense of the larger pattern. It's as simple as this — a sense of witchcraft is as elusive as a sense of humor. It can't be defined or taught. But if you've got it, you know it. You'll know if you belong to us. It's a lovely world full of joy and surprises, rewards beyond imaging.

Prometheus

Seashell Charms

THE OCEAN is an object of awesome beauty and magic. Through ebb and flow, the sea seems to breathe like a pulse or heartbeat. And as Earth bestows precious gems upon us, the ocean provides us with its own gleaming bounty, that of seashells. Such treasures are primordial, and shells are the source of some ancient charms.

During my childhood, we lived in Florida only steps from the ocean. Like most children, the natural spark of magic was alive and well within me. I instinctively knew that there was more to the beach than swimming, playing with pail and shovel, and building sand castles. I adored seashells then, as I still do. Sometimes I would display my thanks by picking flowers and tossing them into the water for the waves to carry off. Then I would wait and wait, hoping for a special shell in return for my gift. Sometimes I would find a shell that day, sometimes not. Either way, I now realize that I was instinctively practicing magic.

I have memories of being lulled to sleep by the sound of the sea, its briny scent mingling with the fragrance of night-blooming jasmine outside my window. And I dreamed a child's dreams of beauty and of magic, so simply activated by gifts from the sea. Many years later I find pleasure in certain seashell charms:

Listening to the sea

Most of us can recall trying to "hear the ocean" by holding a conch shell up to our ears. For people who have psychic powers of clairaudience, the ability to hear outside the range of normal perception, this practice sometimes provides a message. If you are not able to access a direct message, don't give up on the conch shell. Sit quietly in a candlelit room, close your eyes, meditate and hold the shell to your ear. It may or may not have something to say. If not, try it again another time.

Wish manifestation

This charm is beautifully simple. When you need something, begin by finding a shell you like large enough to have writing space on it. Before you proceed, be certain to work with the highest good in mind. Meditate on your need, fixing it clearly in your mind. Once you achieve clarity, etch, paint or ink the wish on the shell's surface. Take the shell to the sea, again pour all your feelings into it, and toss it as hard as you can into the water. The spell is worked. You can also use this technique to "cast something negative out of your life." Just always be careful what you wish for.

To solidify a bond with another person

This takes two willing people. Together, find any bivalve with halves still connected. Use this as you would a wishbone, each of you grasping half the shell. Both instill the same thought or feeling into the shell while holding it. In this case, concentrate on strengthening the connection between you. When the energy reaches its strong point, both pull the halves apart, each retaining half. Keep the shell near you. If you ever desire the bond to end, take your half to the sea, fill it with feeling, and toss it back into the water.

Scrying with the sea

If your psychic talents consist of clairvoyance, here is a way for you to work with shells. Again, if you are not able to actually get to the sea to simply gaze upon her in order to have visions, you can use this seashell method for scrying. You can do this in the same way you would use a crystal ball or other scrying tool. You are simply going to substitute a deep scallop, or clam shell filled with water (sea water, if you like), and gaze into it, waiting for a vision to come. You may facilitate the process by steeping a little mugwort or wormwood in the water prior to pouring it into the shell. If no visions come to you, it does not mean that you will not get any. Just try another time to see what the sea might be ready to reveal to you.

Bright blessings!

– FUSCHIA ROBIN

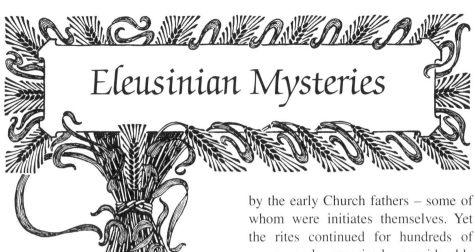

Eleusinian Mysteries

"When Demeter came to our land, in her wandering after the rape of Kore, and being moved to kindness towards our ancestors by services which may not be told except to her initiates, she gave these two gifts, the greatest in the world – the fruits of the earth, which have enabled us to rise above the life of the beasts, and the holy rite, which inspires in those who partake of it sweeter hopes regarding both the end of life and all eternity."

– Panegyricus 4.28, Isocrates

OF THE VARIOUS mystery cults, the ancient Eleusinian Mysteries are possibly the most potent and least well known. The Mysteries, held annually in honor of Demeter and Persephone, were the most sacred of all the Greek ritual celebrations. From all over Greece and later from the Roman Empire, crowds of worshippers gathered to make the pilgrimage between Athens and Eleusis and to participate in the secret ceremonies. As Christianity began to spread, the Mysteries were condemned by the early Church fathers – some of whom were initiates themselves. Yet the rites continued for hundreds of years and exercised considerable influence on the formation of early Christian teaching.

The Eleusinian ceremonies have been kept secret for over two thousand years, although we know that they united the worshipper with the gods and included promises of divine power and rewards in the afterlife. Some of what we understand about the Mysteries come from the ruins of the sanctuary at Eleusis; statues, bas reliefs, and pottery. We have reports from ancient writers such as Aeschylus, Sophocles, Herodotus, Aristophanes, Plutarch, and Pausanias, all of whom were initiates. Accounts have come down to us also from Christian commentators, including Clement of Alexandria. Yet for all this evidence, the true nature of the Mysteries remains shrouded in uncertainty. The participants honored, with remarkable consistency, their pledges not to reveal what took place in the Telesterion, the inner sanctum of the Temple of Demeter. To violate that oath of secrecy was a capital offense.

The Mysteries originated about 1500 BCE and were held annually for about two thousand years. The Homeric Hymn to Demeter relates how King Celeus, one of the deity's original priests, learned the arcane rites and mysteries of her cult. Devotees believed that Triptolemus, the son of Celeus, had learned agrarian techniques from Demeter herself. Around 300 BCE, the state took over the Mysteries under the control of two families, the Eumolpidae and the Keryk.

Four categories of devotees participated in the Eleusinian Mysteries: the priests, priestesses and hierophants; the initiates, undergoing the ceremony for the first time; others who had participated at least once and were eligible for the fourth category; those who had attained *epopteia*, learned the secrets of the greatest mysteries of Demeter. All people, including slaves, were allowed initiation. Only two requirements provided eligibility for membership: a lack of "blood guilt," meaning never having committed murder, and not being a barbarian, meaning unable to speak Greek.

Two Eleusinian Mysteries existed, the Greater and the Lesser. The specifics of their ceremonies remain hidden, but we know that three degrees of initiation occurred: the Lesser Mysteries, a preliminary requirement; the Greater Mysteries or *telete*, "to make perfect"; and the highest degree, the *epopteia*. The *telete* initiation divided into three divisions: the things acted, the things said, and the things shown.

The Mysteries at the Eleusis site revolved around the annual springtime Initiation into the Lesser Mysteries at Agrai, held in March. The priests purified the candidates for initiation, sacrificed a pig to Demeter, then purified themselves. According to Diodorus, the Lesser Mysteries originated for Heracles – Demeter had instituted the ritual in the hero's honor to purify him of guilt for the slaughter of the Centaurs. Initiation into the Greater Mysteries

The Abduction of Persephone   Venice (1501)

67

occurred in early autumn and lasted for nine days. The existing records of these rites show numerous ties to the tale of Demeter and Persephone, told in the Homeric Hymn to Demeter. During this ritual initiates, or *mystai*, drank the *kykeon*, experiencing an illuminating vision which transformed them into *epoptai*, "those who had seen".

Scholars disagree widely over the significance of the *kykeon*. Some have maintained that it must have had a sacramental character involving a communion with the deity or assimilation of the deity's spirit. Another scholar believes that the drinking of the *kykeon* was an "act of religious remembrance" involving "an observance of an act of the Goddess." Even on this scant evidence similarity to the Christian Eucharist arises. As to the sacred drink, apparently it was not alcoholic, since the Homeric Hymn states that Demeter did not partake of wine. Yet it has been suggested that there might have been an admixture of other intoxicating ingredients. Joseph Campbell, for example, has speculated that the grains of wheat may have contained small quantities of ergot, a natural hallucinogen sometimes occurring in cereal base. The Mysteries were based around the legend of Demeter and the search for her missing daughter, Persephone. According to the Homeric Hymn to Demeter:

"Apart from Demeter, lady of the golden sword and glorious fruits, she was playing with the deep-bosomed daughters of Oceanus and gathering flowers over a soft meadow, roses and crocuses and beautiful violets, irises also and hyacinths and the narcissus, which Earth made to grow at the will of Zeus and to please the Host of Many, to be a snare for the bloom-like girl – a marvelous, radiant flower. It was a thing of awe whether for deathless gods or mortal men to see: from its root grew a hundred blooms and it smelled most sweetly, so that all wide heaven above and the whole earth and the sea's salt swell laughed for joy. And the girl was amazed and reached out with both hands to take the lovely toy; but the wide-pathed earth yawned there in the plain of Nysa, and the lord, Host of Many, with his immortal horses sprang out upon her – the Son of Cronos, He who has many names. He caught her up reluctant on his golden car and bore her away lamenting. Then she cried out shrilly with her voice, calling upon her father, the Son of Cronos, who is most high and excellent."

Hades and Persephone dining

Demeter searched high and low for Persephone. In her distress, the grieving goddess neglected her agricultural duties and a terrible dry season descended on earth. Finally, by consulting Zeus, Demeter was reunited with her daughter and the earth returned to its former fruitfulness. Unfortunately Persephone was unable to remain in the land of the living. In the underworld she had consumed four pomegranate seeds Hades had tricked her into eating. Those who eat the food of the dead may not return to the living world. But an agreement was effected, and Persephone promised to stay in the underworld with Hades one month of the year for each seed that she had eaten and with her mother the remaining eight months of the year.

The Eleusinian Mysteries celebrated Persephone's return, for it was also the return of plants and of life to the earth. She had gone into the underworld (underground, like seeds in the winter), and returned to the land of the living. Her rebirth is therefore symbolic of the rebirth of all plant life during the spring, and by extension all life on earth.

In 392 CE the Mysteries were suppressed by the Roman emperor Theodosius I, who closed the sanctuaries in an effort to destroy pagan resistance to Christianity as a state religion. The last remnants of the Mysteries were wiped out four years later when the Goths invaded, led by Alaric accompanied by Christians "in their dark garments." With them they brought Arian Christianity and the desecration of the old sacred sites. The demise of the Eleusinian Mysteries is reported by Eunapios, a historian and biographer of the Greek philosophers. Eunapios had been initiated by the last legitimate hierophant, commissioned by the emperor Julian to restore the Mysteries. According to Eunapios, the very last hierophant was a usurper, "the man from Thespiai who held the rank of Father in the mysteries of Mithras."

The Eleusinian Mysteries have provided inspiration for the modern neopagan movement. The New Reformed Orthodox Order of the Golden Dawn and the Aquarian Tabernacle Church hold an annual reenactment of the Mysteries – and have also inspired countless other visionaries in the contemporary world. The Homeric Hymn to Demeter assures us that, "Happy is he among men upon earth who has seen these mysteries."

– ASH MCSHEE

69

Crop Circles

Hoax, mystery or message?

FOR DECADES CROP circles have caught the imagination of occultists, conspiracy theorists, and others interested in mysterious events. Where the circles appear, wheat, barley and similar plants are flattened in a spiral pattern at the base. The crop circles vary from a few yards in diameter to huge formations completely visible only from the air – but all give the impression of great power and precision.

Although these patterns of crushed plants became widely observed in the 1970s, similar phenomena have been known for centuries. A seventeenth-century woodcut, "The Mowing Devil," depicts a strange creature creating a circular design in a field, and Scandinavian folklore speaks of elves creating circles in wheat. Shortly after World War II, an aerial survey of Britain revealed circular patterns of various crops, and investigation of these formations led to the discovery of significant archaeological sites.

But crop circles, as we recognize them today, came into prominence in 1972. Two Englishmen, Bryce Bond and Arthur Shuttlewood, were the first to witness a circle being formed. They spoke of "a great imprint taking shape" in front of them. Mystics and skeptics alike took interest. Some of the latter attributed the circles to freak weather conditions, others to soil problems. In 1980, the appearance of two symmetrical circles in a U.K. field dealt a major blow to proponents of both theories.

More complicated patterns appeared over the years, heightening public interest in crop circles. Skeptics continued to blame weather, soil, and pranksters; those inclined toward alternative explanations looked to mystical energy or alien messages.

The debate took a new turn in 1991, when Doug Bower and Dave Chorley revealed that they had been making crop circles since 1978, using common household tools. Some people claim that this admission explains all crop circles. Since Bower and Chorley admitted to producing complex patterns which could fool observers, they say, all crop circles could have been pranks, and probably were. Others believe that the situation is less easily explained. For one thing, they ask, if Bower and Chorley started their hoax in 1978, what explains the crop circles in the six previous years? Were these formations all pranks? And, if so, what inspired people to start playing them?

Other evidence also prevails against the hoax theory. People who study crop circles – half-jokingly called "cerealogists" – point out that the wheat or barley in many circles bend just below the joint. This wouldn't happen in manmade circles, they say. Instead, the stems would crack. Scientific studies on nodes at the plant's apex seem to support this point. Similarly, when circles appear in seed-bearing crops, the seed pods are usually unbroken, whereas people trampling crops would crush the pods. Skeptics say that it's possible with sufficient care to avoid breakage; others remain unconvinced.

If crop circles aren't all the product of human pranksters, what does cause them? Theories abound. One is that the patterns in crop circles are the result of sound vibrations, with the patterns growing more complex as the sounds grow higher. Some people also believe that a satellite produces the patterns via a heat ray, and the crop damage does resemble that which would be produced by high-intensity microwave radiation. However, the crops themselves show no signs of radiation, adding yet another element of mystery to the situation.

As is frequently the case with unexplained events, many people attribute crop circles to alien visitors. The crop circles, they say, may actually be the imprint of flying saucers left when alien pilots visit Earth for abduction or observation. Others think that the circles are deliberate, and that if we could interpret the patterns we would find a message to guide humanity into the next millennium.

In addition to these explanations, some people believe that crop circles are caused by mystical forces. They cite the frequency with which the circles occur near well-known mystical sites. Crop circles in southern England have appeared near earth barrows, stone circles and white chalk hillside designs, all considered ancient sites of mystical activity.

It is easy to be skeptical about crop circles, to say that the hoaxes disprove the reality. But to reject such cynicism is to recognize the many mysteries present in all of daily life.

Those who can embrace the unknown and unknowable, both in themselves and in the wider world, recognize that there is more to crop circles than we understand. Perhaps this deeper meaning will be revealed someday – or perhaps crop circles will remain one of our constant enigmas.

– Isabel Kunkle

Nightmare Phantoms
Something evil this way comes?

TO LIE SUPINE in the yogic tradition is known as Savasana, or corpse pose. As the name indicates, this fundamental posture is conceived to give the practitioner a closeness with death, to be placed on the ground like a corpse. The theory goes that if you learn to die while still alive, you will overcome the fear of death. Savasana demands stillness, encourages meditation, and deeply relaxes muscles. Sometimes the novice practitioner falls asleep during Savasana, the deep relaxation of both body and mind proving hard to resist. When we recall that Sleep and Death are referred to as "twin brothers" in Greek mythology, it follows that sleep, like Savasana, serves to bring the student even closer to death.

But the closer people come to death, to the thin gateway of the netherworlds, the closer we come to the beings intent on pulling us through to the other side. For centuries, it seems, these malevolent entities have been visiting us as we sleep – history is replete with accounts of vicious nocturnal attacks. Like the Old Hag of Newfoundland, who pounds her victims breasts with both fists until

their lungs are void of air. Or the incubi of eighteenth-century Europe, who lay with women as they sleep, conscious of the attack but unable to defend themselves. Or Kokma, the spirits of dead babies that haunt certain areas of the West Indies, leaping on their paralyzed victims' chests and clutching at their throats. Or the Tsog Tsuam of Laos, the Greek Ephialtes, the German Hexendruken, the Russian Kikimora, and on and on. The spirits come in many forms and are known by many names, but their assaults are the same. They come while you're asleep, paralyze your body, then do with you as they please.

But are these really malevolent otherworldly beings that come to us in the night or does something else come into play? For skeptics, these accounts are easy to dismiss as mere superstition. But for people who have been plagued

Death, from the engraving Knight, Death and Devil, *by Albrecht Dürer, 1513*

by these demonic images, dismissal is next to impossible. Recently, however, an explanation has been offered by science that may begin to satisfy both skeptics and believers. For science, these bizarre nocturnal attacks by supernatural beings are expressions of an equally bizarre phenomenon known as sleep paralysis, or SP. During REM sleep, the brain shuts off the body's ability to move, preventing sleepers from acting out potentially dangerous dreams. Sleep paralysis occurs when sleepers waken but bodily movements remain inhibited. Sleepers are conscious, they can open and move their eyes, but their bodies are still asleep.

Sleep paralysis occurs in two forms, CSP and HSP, and almost always strike while sleepers are on their backs. Common sleep paralysis, or CSP, is characterized by an inability to move or speak for 30 seconds to three minutes just before falling asleep or just after waking up. Most people experience CSP at least once in their lives, but for some the event is recurrent. HSP, or hallucinatory sleep paralysis, is more rare. HSP is characterized by the inability to move or speak for a longer duration of time, usually seven to eight minutes.

 In this state hallucinations appear as the sleeper either falls asleep or wakes up. These hallucinations can be auditory, visual, or tactile, and may affect the sensory receptors that detect the movement and placement of the body.

Once people experience the type of hallucinatory sensations generated by HSP, demons do indeed seem the natural culprit. Subjects report intense fear associated with the episodes, linked to the sensing of an evil presence just out of sight, pressure on their chests or even the sensation of being choked. Victims can feel as though they are pulled out of bed, pushed through the bed, or floating above the bed. These sensations can be accompanied by unexplained lights or intense sounds, such as buzzing or ringing. For sleepers experiencing HSP, the phenomenon has a tangible quality, as real or more so than anything encountered in waking life.

But perhaps the most bizarre, most troubling aspect of HSP (and most difficult to account for scientifically) is the feeling of impending death that is frequently reported. It seems that whatever presence lurks just out of sight wants to rip the dreamer's life away. The feeling is so intense, so convincing that subjects feel the need to fight with all their might. The fight is usually fruitless, and when dreamers regain the ability to move, the shock usually keeps them still.

Though "unusual," this feeling has been reported for centuries from every corner of the globe. In China, household cats were known to steal a sleeping person's breath. In ancient Japan, the phenomenon was credited to mischievous spectral foxes. Today, the phenomenon is called *kanashibari*, which means "bound by iron ropes" and is a well known and accepted experience in the culture, though still terrifying. In Judeo-Christian mythology the culprits are fallen angels who guard sleeping women. The "watchers" sometimes become overwhelmed by lust and succumb to temptation, ravishing those they were meant to protect. The offspring of these unions are said to roam the earth, claiming more victims with their lust. Even people of secular countries such as ours who lack a common mythos to explain the experience regularly report episodes of HSP. It has even been suggested that bedside alien abductions are simply our culture's unique interpretation of HSP – which would account for the fact that alien abductions never occur in nearby Canada or Mexico.

The science concerning sleep paralysis is still relatively new, with research only a few decades old. For more than two thousand years the hallucinations generated by HSP have been credited to otherworldly beings. And like many of history's unexplained, unpleasant occurrences, witches have borne the blame. From Mexico, Newfoundland, Ireland, Scotland and England all come stories of witches who attack in the dead of night. This stigma endures even today, with the terms "sleep paralysis" and "Old Hag Phenomenon" used interchangeably within the research communities. But science has yet to give us a satisfying answer for why this phenomenon occurs. We understand the how of it; we understand the biological mechanics involved. But what causes these mechanisms to malfunction? What can account for the feeling of impending death or the sense that something evil is standing just inches away? How can such a real experience be an illusion?

Perhaps the answer lies not in what science can tell us, but in our beginning, in Savasana. The closeness with death cultivated by this pose not only eases our fear, but can open a gateway to higher levels of consciousness. Mastery of this deceptively simple posture can lead to a feeling of freedom, of floating, of an utterly clear and undiluted perception of the world. No longer bound by terror, the yoga practitioner can tap into something eternal. HSP can be a guide to wonderfully pleasant experiences such as Lucid Dreaming, in which the sleeper consciously navigates the dreamscape with perfect recall of out-of-body experiences or astral travel. Once we can move past the initial fear and decide not to fight, the same gateway can lead us from terror to a blissfully different experience.

– SHANNON MARKS

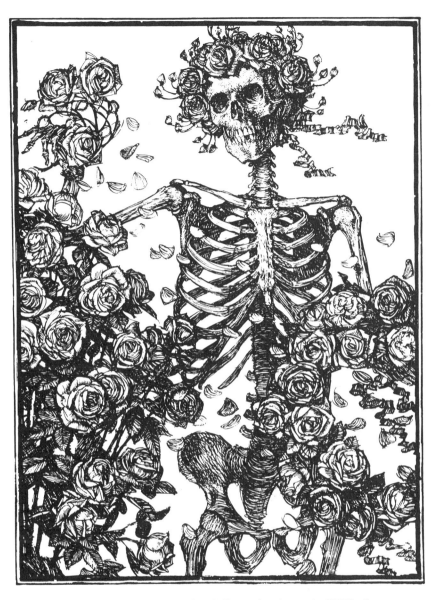

Illustration by Edmund J. Sullivan for Quatrain XXVI of
The Rubáiyát of Omar Khayyám, *by Edward Fitzgerald, London, 1859.*

Oh, come with old Khayyám, and leave the Wise
To talk; one thing is certain, that Life flies;
One thing is certain, and the Rest is Lies;
The Flower that once has blown forever dies.

Moon Cycles

A New Moon rises with the Sun,
Her waxing half at midday shows,
The Full Moon climbs at sunset hour,
And waning half the midnight knows.

NEW	2008	FULL	NEW	2009	FULL
January 8		January 22	January 26		January 10
February 6		February 20	February 24		February 9
March 7		March 21	March 26		March 10
April 5		April 20	April 24		April 9
May 5		May 19	May 24		May 9
June 3		June 18	June 22		June 7
July 2		July 18	July 21		July 7
August 1/30		August 16	August 20		August 5
September 29		September 15	September 18		September 4
October 28		October 14	October 18		October 4
November 27		November 13	November 16		November 2
December 27		December 12	December 16		December 2/31

Life takes on added dimension when you match your activities to the waxing and waning of the Moon.
Observe the sequence of her phases to learn the wisdom of constant change within complete certainty.

presage

by Dikki-Jo Mullen

ARIES 2007 — PISCES 2008

During the year to come, the planet Pluto will conjoin the Galactic Center. Pluto then moves ahead to the cusp of Capricorn, making a rare, once-in-a-generation sign change in early 2008. The last time Pluto was in Capricorn the Declaration of Independence was being signed. The Galactic Center relates to spiritual aspirations, the equilibrium of power, and individual influence over the environment. Pluto is the planetary transformer. Capricorn rules security, structure, the land, and responsibility. The message from the universe is to expect changing values both politically and economically. It's important to remain flexible and tolerant. Be of good courage and good cheer. In many ways we will soon be welcomed by a very different world.

Autumn eclipses in Pisces and Virgo emphasize wellness, diet, and the care of the water supply. Late winter eclipses in Aquarius and Virgo point to new technology and political shifts. From September through the Yule season and again at winter's end Mars makes a long transit through Cancer. Preserving places of historical interest, comfortable housing, and heritage will become priorities. From early June through early October Venus retrogrades in and out of Leo. Interesting celebrity news, avant garde trends in the arts, and exceptionally talented young people will be a focus. Dramatic expressions of love and generosity during this time will touch the hearts of many. Saturn shifts into Virgo for a two-year stay on September 2. This accents healthy foods and lifestyles. The trend encourages "de-cluttering," enhancing your surroundings for greater efficiency and simplicity.

If you know your Moon and Ascendant, or rising sign, check the segments related to those as well as your familiar birth or Sun Sign. Presage reveals how to follow the path set in the stars and find the brightest, best personal journey during the year to come.

ASTROLOGICAL KEYS

Signs of the Zodiac
Channels of Expression

ARIES: fiery, pioneering, competitive
TAURUS: earthy, stable, practical
GEMINI: dual, lively, versatile
CANCER: protective, traditional
LEO: dramatic, flamboyant, warm
VIRGO: conscientious, analytical
LIBRA: refined, fair, sociable
SCORPIO: intense, secretive, ambitious
SAGITTARIUS: friendly, expansive
CAPRICORN: cautious, materialistic
AQUARIUS: inquisitive, unpredictable
PISCES: responsive, dependent, fanciful

Elements

FIRE: Aries, Leo, Sagittarius
EARTH: Taurus, Virgo, Capricorn
AIR: Gemini, Libra, Aquarius
WATER: Cancer, Scorpio, Pisces

Qualities

CARDINAL	FIXED	MUTABLE
Aries	Taurus	Gemini
Cancer	Leo	Virgo
Libra	Scorpio	Sagittarius
Capricorn	Aquarius	Pisces

CARDINAL signs mark the beginning of each new season — active.
FIXED signs represent the season at its height — steadfast.
MUTABLE signs herald a change of season — variable.

Celestial Bodies
Generating Energy of the Cosmos

Sun: birth sign, ego, identity
Moon: emotions, memories, personality
Mercury: communication, intellect, skills
Venus: love, pleasures, the fine arts
Mars: energy, challenges, sports
Jupiter: expansion, religion, happiness
Saturn: responsibility, maturity, realities
Uranus: originality, science, progress
Neptune: dreams, illusions, inspiration
Pluto: rebirth, renewal, resources

Glossary of Aspects

Conjunction: two planets within the same sign or less than 10 degrees apart, favorable or unfavorable according to the nature of the planets.

Sextile: a pleasant, harmonious aspect occurring when two planets are two signs or 60 degrees apart.

Square: a major negative effect resulting when planets are three signs from one another or 90 degrees apart.

Trine: planets four signs or 120 degrees apart, forming a positive and favorable influence.

Quincunx: a mildly negative aspect produced when planets are five signs or 150 degrees apart.

Opposition: a six sign or 180 degrees separation of planets generating positive or negative forces depending on the planets involved.

The Houses — *Twelve Areas of Life*

1st house: appearance, image, identity
2nd house: money, possessions, tools
3rd house: communications, siblings
4th house: family, domesticity, security
5th house: romance, creativity, children
6th house: daily routine, service, health
7th house: marriage, partnerships, union
8th house: passion, death, rebirth, soul
9th house: travel, philosophy, education
10th house: fame, achievement, mastery
11th house: goals, friends, high hopes
12th house: sacrifice, solitude, privacy

ECLIPSES

Few celestial phenomena have generated the awe that an eclipse does. Inspirational, terrifying, and intriguing, eclipses are linked to the unpredictable. Extend a welcome embrace to change when an eclipse takes place.

Eclipses conjoining the north node of the Moon are thought to be more favorable than those conjunct the south node.

The most significant eclipses occur within three days of the birthday. The clever mystic will reflect and observe rather than act during an eclipse. Eclipses bring upheaval during the three months before they occur and throughout the year afterward. This coming year brings four eclipses.

August 28	Full Moon Lunar in Pisces, north node – total
September 11	New Moon Solar in Virgo, south node – partial
February 7	New Moon Solar in Aquarius, north node – partial
February 20	Full Moon Lunar in Virgo, south node – total

PLANETS IN RETROGRADE MOTION

Regroup, revisit, reflect, reconnect, revamp are all words starting with the prefix "re," as does the word "retrograde." That's the secret to understanding how retrograde motion works in astrology. The retrograde motion is an optical illusion created by the planet's motion relative to the Earth's orbital speed. However, the impact of a planetary retrograde is very genuine. Fate offers a second chance, the established order is changing. Matters ruled by the retrograde planet are involved.

Mercury Retrograde Cycles

Mercury's retrograde cycles occur more often than those of other planets and augur delayed travel and confused communication. Expect contact from associates who have been out of touch. Remain in familiar territory, confirm plans, and complete ongoing projects. Avoid moving your residence or starting a different job while Mercury is retrograde. The changes will be marred by delays and frustrations. Be cautious about signing contracts, all is not as it seems. Retrograde Mercury cycles are great for past life study, reunions, and exploring historical sites. Geminis and Virgos, who are ruled by Mercury, notice this trend the most.
6/16 – 7/10, 2007 in Cancer;
10/12–11/2, 2007 in Scorpio and Libra;
1/29, 2008 – 2/19, 2008 in Aquarius

Venus Retrograde Cycle

Venus is the rarest retrograde. Postpone changes in personal commitments, especially marital status. Keep a sense of humor if someone exhibits bad manners or dresses inappropriately. Tolerate diverse taste in the fine arts. Legal matters can go awry. Taurus and Libra, who are ruled by Venus, especially respond to this influence.
7/28–9/9, 2007 in Virgo and Leo

Mars Retrograde Cycle

Aggressive actions are not successful. There can be a focus on sports figures, the military, and heavy industry. The Mars-ruled and co-ruled signs, Aries and Scorpio, are impacted the most.
11/16, 2007 – 1/31, 2008 in Cancer and Gemini

ARIES

The year ahead for those
born under the sign of the Ram
March 20–April 19

Forever rushing, leaping, and charging ahead with force, the rambunctious Ram parades at the front of the zodiac, awakening the sleeping world to the excitement of another spring. Aries links to vigor and exploration and is the pure, bright flame of spirit teaching the lessons of courage.

Friends are confused and confusing during spring's early days. Your ruling planet, Mars, dashes with Neptune in the 11th house. Keep peer pressure in perspective near All Fool's Day. An uncharacteristic subtlety prevails from the vernal equinox to April 6 when Mars joins Uranus in Pisces in your 12th house. Dreams and visions are prevalent. Mid-April finds Mercury moving quickly through your sign. It's a marvelous time for travel, correspondence, and study programs. Near Beltane finances are favored. At the same time Jupiter and Saturn form a perfect trine in your sister fire signs of Sagittarius and Leo. An income-producing scheme becomes fruitful. By May 16 Mars enters your sign where it remains through Midsummer's Day. Mars completes a grand trine in the fire signs with Saturn and Jupiter, making late spring and early summer a time to take advantage of high energy.

In July retrograde Mercury in Cancer entangles the Sun in your 4th house in a square aspect. Family members might be at odds; a residential move can be considered. After July 10 the way becomes clearer. Listen with your heart and read between the lines if someone close to you isn't easy to understand. At Lammastide Saturn is strongly aspected to Mars and impacts your 5th house. Be patient with younger people and creative projects. By August 8 Jupiter completes a retrograde in your 9th house. Fire rituals of all kinds offer focus and inspiration. The mutable eclipses on August 28 and September 11 accent your personal health as well as your own abilities as a healer. Be receptive to new healing techniques—a special animal companion may be involved. Celebrate the Full Moon of September 26. It falls in Aries and is applying to a wide trine with Venus in Leo. Your sector of romance and pleasure is highlighted. Accept and issue invitations.

During October, Cancer and Libra transits including Mars, the Sun, and a retrograde Mercury aspect your angular houses. Immediate attention must be paid to partnership and family needs. Double-check all legal documents for accuracy. A friend from the past makes contact near Halloween. During meditation, a past life recollection is helpful. November finds Mars turning retrograde, a pattern which will be in effect until the end of January. A new perspective on your childhood as well as insight into the family tree can come about quite unexpectedly. During December Venus creates a promising influence in your 8th house while making a series of favorable trine and sextile aspects to water and earth sign planets. Invested or inherited funds can add to your financial security. Matters linked to insurance coverage can be resolved in a satisfactory manner. This culminates on the Full Moon of December 23.

January opens with retrograde Mars entering Gemini where it favorably aspects Neptune in Aquarius. Your 3rd and 11th houses are highlighted. Friends suggest travel plans. An urge to make a change for the better and crusade against old wrongs prevails. Candlemas marks Pluto's entry into Capricorn, your career sector. A time of transformation linked to your path of fame and fortune approaches. Be receptive to changing patterns in your industry. February's eclipses promise a change of heart. Your sectors of love, pleasure, and friendship, the 5th and 11th houses, are impacted. During March family matters need attention, for Mars in Cancer squares your Sun. Complete needed maintenance on your dwelling, and be tolerant if the very young or the elderly in your extended family reveal a cantankerous side.

HEALTH

The eclipse of September 11 falls in your 6th house of health. It's a wonderful time to explore new health care strategies. Establish a closer link with the earth. While Mars is retrograde November 16 – January 31 examine habits and patterns. Perform a fire or smudging ceremony to help you release all that is counterproductive. This includes toxic relationships as well as habits. A sachet of dragon's blood with a bloodstone can be carried to enhance your resolve and strength.

LOVE

For the past couple of years Saturn has been in your love sector, creating disappointments regarding matters of the heart. In September a more promising time begins. The Harvest Moon on September 26 shines brightly in your sign, ushering in a four-week cycle when your charm is at a peak. Draw down the Moon by lighting nine candles just as the Sun sets. Choose tapers in the corals, reds, and golds of the autumn season.

SPIRITUALITY

Pluto is completing a long transit through your sector of spirituality. You've undergone some radical transformations in your beliefs for more than a decade. Review your spiritual journey; examine where you're going. It's a time to release practices which no longer inspire you. A past life regression near the winter solstice helps integrate your spiritual experiences from past incarnations into your current beliefs.

FINANCE

Venus transits your 2nd house of earnings in early spring. A friend could help you maximize financial opportunities. Combine business with pleasure from late March through mid-April. Just after the summer solstice through Lammastide a powerful Mars tie impacts finances. You'll be motivated to work harder, but don't let anger regarding finances develop. Prepare a prosperity talisman by binding a teaspoon each of coriander and allspice along with a cabochon of green quartz in a square of gold cloth. Place it in your workplace or carry it in your wallet.

TAURUS

The year ahead for those
born under the sign of the Bull
April 20 – May 20

Persistent and strong-willed, yet affectionate, this fixed sign of Earth provides security and nurture. The Bull can be possessive and, obviously, quite stubborn. However, no one will be more reliable and loyal once a bond is forged.

Love, laughter, and beauty greet you as Venus dances through your sign through April 11. Late April finds Saturn completing a retrograde in your home and family sector. Old issues about residence and relatives can be resolved. Your birthday month finds Mercury moving rapidly through Taurus. Travel plans and opportunities are available. Your mental energy will be in top form; it's especially easy to assimilate new information. Beltane is ideal for consecrating a new journal. You have much to express. From early June through Midsummer's Day a grand trine in the fire signs highlights your 4th, 8th, and 12th houses. Meditate on the past, then release that which no longer serves you. This is a time when visualizations can manifest. Be certain to build only positive thought forms.

Mars enters your sign on June 24 and remains there through August 7. You'll feel enthused and motivated, but must direct anger and impatience into positive outlets. Near Independence Day and at Lammastide you'll be especially forceful and competitive. Venus is retrograde July 28 – September 9. Your 4th and 5th houses are impacted. An old flame can be rekindled. Go slowly with forming serious commitments or changing an existing relationship. The eclipse of August 28 brings a new goal to consider. As the autumn equinox approaches, Mars and Jupiter are strongly aspected in your financial sectors, the 2nd and 8th houses. This brings out the gambler in you. Consider any risky investments carefully.

October finds Venus in Virgo, your sister earth sign, favorably affecting your sector of pleasure. Develop a new hobby; express your deepest feelings. The Full Moon on October 25, just before Samhain, shines in your sign. Your psychic ability and personal charisma are at a peak. Follow your heart and intuition; accept and issue invitations. Early November brings a quincunx from Mercury in your health sector. Be certain that your diet is balanced and drink plenty of pure water or healthful teas and juices. Get routine medical checkups scheduled by November 12. Mid-November finds Mars beginning a six-week retrograde cycle in your 2nd and 3rd houses. Correct problems related to transportation. Adopt a tolerant attitude with any difficult neighbors or siblings. On December 5 Venus crosses into your 7th house where it remains through Yuletide. This is a perfect cycle for resolving any legal issues that need attention. A partner is loving and thoughtful. Devote the winter solstice eve to honoring teamwork and sharing.

January begins with a stellium of planets including the Sun, Mercury, Venus, and Jupiter gathering in your 9th house. It's a time to explore. At Candlemas retrograde Mercury conjoins Neptune in your 10th house. Preserve the status quo at work. Temporarily, there is great confusion about career direction. Gaze into a crystal or consult the Tarot for insight. Take note if a dream is sent, but interpret the symbols carefully. A change made in haste now could lead to regret. The eclipses of February 6 and 20 will highlight new factors coming into play. Wait and watch until the month's end. Move forward after February 21. On March 5 a helpful Mars transit begins in your 11th house. Friends express concern and make an effort to include you in plans. On March 13 Venus changes signs. Through winter's end you'll experience deeper love and acceptance. The New Moon on March 7 brings enthusiasm about new goals. Politics are intriguing. You'll be embraced by a deeper spirit of community and altruism. Reach out to new friends.

HEALTH

The throat, ears, and thyroid are especially linked to your birth sign. Protect your neck from cold drafts with an attractive scarf. A series of yoga postures (the shoulder stand followed by the plough and the fish) can be very helpful in equalizing the thyroid gland. Venus rules both your 6th house of health and your birth sign overall. While Venus is retrograde July 28–September 9 be aware of which health habits should be changed. Focus on reaching the perfect weight and on dental care.

LOVE

On September 3 Saturn begins a two-and-a-half-year passage through your 5th house of romance and pleasure. There will be an awareness of what is or is not feasible in the love department. Accept a rejection philosophically and be patient. Fulfillment of romantic dreams can require time and effort now. A beloved needs extra tender loving care. Give generously and there will be rewards in the long run. Tend a witch's garden of traditional love herbs, including catnip, thyme, and verbena. As the seedlings grow and mature, love prospects will multiply.

SPIRITUALITY

Pluto begins a rare sign change during late winter, moving into Capricorn, your 9th house of spirituality. This inaugurates a deep catharsis, marking a transformation in your faith which will unfold for years to come. You'll question old concepts and seek new, deeper levels of truth. The Full Moon of June 30 can bring a hint of the specifics. Hold deeply colored crystals such as lapis lazuli, amethyst, and emerald while in meditation. Listen for the voice of the Green Man while outdoors.

FINANCE

This should be a promising cycle for finances. Jupiter, the celestial ruler of luck and wealth, transits your 8th house through December 18. Income from an investment, tax, insurance, or estate settlement can add to your earnings. Early 2008 finds a cluster of planets in your sister earth signs of Capricorn and Virgo. Ease and stability are building. You'll discover the route to true security.

GEMINI
The year ahead for those
born under the sign of the Twins
May 21–June 20

Changeable, restless, inquisitive, and lively, Gemini always makes life interesting. This first of the mutable and first of the air signs, Gemini's twin spirit seeks variety. You brush away the cobwebs of habit to express and explore new ideas.

Spring dawns with Mercury, your ruler, moving rapidly through your career sector. Through April 10 you'll be arranging meetings and exchanging calls and letters. Since Mercury conjoins Uranus, innovations and surprises may develop. A sense of déjà vu infuses relationships when Jupiter turns retrograde in your 7th house of partners in early April, a pattern which lasts through Lammastide. Associates have new priorities. Compromises can be reached when benevolent Venus transits Gemini from mid-April through May 8. Orient magical workings on May Day to the blessing of compatible relationships. The last three weeks of May bring important answers when Mercury trines sensitive Neptune and intuition marches with intellect.

During June, Venus joins Saturn in Leo to create a sextile aspect in the 3rd house. At the New Moon in Gemini on June 14 business travel should be productive. Retrograde Mercury in Cancer June 16–July 10 creates some confusion about budgeting and finances. A sentimental mood prevails. Venus is retrograde at a square to your Sun from late July through September 8. Economize in regard to expenses as well as the outpouring of emotion and energy. From early August through the end of September Mars dashes through Gemini. It's easy to be a bit abrupt. Moderate exercise and good-natured competition provide positive outlets for anger. A series of squares and oppositions creates a complex aspect pattern in mutable signs with Mars as the pivot. It's an interesting time, but stress can build. Take time to focus and keep your goals in mind. Then much can be accomplished.

During October, Venus moves with Saturn through your home and family sector. Repair and redecorate your dwelling, then host a gathering at All Hallows. Emphasize talismans to bring peace, joy, and protection to the home. An elderly or very young relative can become a closer companion. The New Moon of November 9 ushers in a two-week cycle accenting the 6th house. Health could be affected by changes in diet. Emotional bonds with animal companions, especially canines, can strengthen. November 24's Full Moon in your sign widely aspects both Venus and Neptune. Social prospects are bright; your charm and artistic gifts are in evidence through the month's end.

The first half of December finds the Sun, Mercury, Jupiter, and Pluto all in opposition to you. It's essential to understand others' viewpoints and capacities. Ask no favors, and release expectations. Water, snow, and ice magic will be powerful at Yule. Venus in Scorpio complements other water sign influences, including Uranus in Pisces and Mars in Cancer. January finds Jupiter and Pluto starting long transits through Capricorn, activating your 8th house, the sector of transformation, mysteries, and the afterlife. Efforts to contact a loved one who has passed on can be very successful. At Candlemas select individual tapers and light them, dedicating each candle to a specific change desired as Mars turns direct in your sign. It's time to move on.

February's eclipses, on the 6th and the 20th, create a stir in the 9th and 4th houses. A family member may announce some unexpected plans. Be understanding and supportive. March accents security issues, for Mars in Cancer is powerfully aspected in your 2nd house of finances. Balancing old monetary obligations with current expenses requires humor and tolerance. During winter's final days check the claims and references of associates with care. Mercury conjoins first Neptune, then Uranus, showing that reality is in flux. Clouds of confusion clear in good time.

HEALTH

Mars makes two passages through Gemini this year, during August and September and again January 1–March 4. This brings the gift of great energy, but also warns of building stress and anger. Focus on regular exercise as a release. It's the perfect time to begin a healthful regime of Pranayama, the yoga of sacred breath work. Seek out a yoga studio or textbook for specifics and you'll be rewarded with a new wellness and strength by the year's end.

LOVE

Good communication skills open your heart to romance. A classroom or educational tour could provide opportunities. Venus makes promising aspects April, November, and late February through mid-March. An encounter with Cupid is likely then. Lemongrass and bergamot are favorable aromatherapies. A feng shui technique suggests placing new peach or pink sheets on your bed to attract true love. This should be effective within twenty-eight days, one lunar cycle.

SPIRITUALITY

The Aquarius eclipse of February 6 profoundly impacts your spirituality. It aspects Neptune, the planet of dreams, which hovers in your spiritual sector the year long. Dreams usher in spiritual revelations. Invest in a good dream book. The eclipse marks the onset of Chinese New Year. This is a perfect time to learn more about the traits of your own Chinese birth sign. Obtain a statue or make a drawing of your Chinese animal. Gaze upon it, for it is the animal that hides within your heart.

FINANCE

Pluto, the celestial transformer, is about to touch the cusp of Capricorn, your 8th house. Old beliefs about money are changing. Favorable aspects between Jupiter and Saturn in earth signs in early 2008 should activate the higher potentials of this Pluto trend, brightening financial prospects between Yule and Candlemas. Promote financial plans between the First Quarter and Full Moon phases each month. Your teaching ability can also enhance earnings.

CANCER

The year ahead for those
born under the sign of the Crab
June 21–July 22

Kindly, sympathetic and very sensitive, the Crab is always responsive. This second of the cardinal and first of the water signs offers emotional support to others. Driven by moods and feelings, you have a special affinity with the ever-changing Moon and tides.

Friendship is the keynote of early spring. A Venus sextile brightens your 11th house through April 11. Ask advice from and offer assistance to companions about setting goals and pursuing dreams. Your energy level will be wonderful April 7–May 15 for Mars joins Uranus, and both trine your Sun. Nurture your confidence and be adventurous. Much can be accomplished near May Eve. Honor the sabbat by combining fire with water. Mid-May through June 5 Venus makes a very rapid transit through your sign. Focus on creative projects. Love and social prospects are changing for the better. Don't hesitate if someone new has caught your eye. Make your feelings known. Old friends reconnect near the summer solstice. Mercury is retrograde in your sign, a trend which lasts until July 10. It's a sentimental cycle. July 11–August 9 favors a journey. Mercury will be direct again and very well aspected. The New Moon in Cancer on July 14 is an excellent time to make decisions about study and travel. Lammastide finds Venus retrograde in your sector of siblings and neighbors. Be tolerant if one of them is not as considerate as you'd like, there might be deeper issues involved. Contemplate romantic options carefully, but don't change your relationship status until after September 9.

The eclipses of August 28 and September 11 emphasize communication and learning. Write a poem or start a journal. A different spiritual perspective can have appeal, for your 9th house of faith and philosophy is highlighted. At the autumnal equinox Venus forms several favorable aspects in your financial sector. Pursue opportunities to add to your income; a friend may suggest valuable contacts or ideas concerning your earning power. The Full Moon on September 26 brightens your 10th house of fame and fortune.

As October begins, Mars crosses into your sign and stays until New Year's Eve. You'll be much more assertive than usual. Control confrontational urges; use this gift of added energy constructively. In early November, Mercury changes direction in your home and family sector. New ideas about your residence and changing goals voiced by relatives have to be considered. Focus on clear communication with loved ones; make a decision about a move after November 3.

From November 12–December 1 Mercury forms a grand trine in water signs, involving both Mars and Uranus. This is extremely favorable for travel, writing, conversation, and study. December finds Mars in the midst of a retrograde which impacts you profoundly. Release old anger, memories, or habits which no longer serve you. Meditate on self-understanding beneath the light of the Full Moon in Cancer on December 23. Relationships are marked by expansion. Jupiter is starting a yearlong passage in Capricorn, your marriage and partnership sector, late in December. This promises growth and new horizons. The first week of January brings a Sun-Mercury opposition to your sign. Encourage others to talk. Work out compromises, and all will be well. Candlemas features a stellium of Aquarius planets, including Neptune, in your 8th house. This aspects Mars in Gemini in your 12th house. A deeper awareness of the afterlife develops. February favors quiet reverie, past life regression, and connecting with the spirit world. In March, Mars crosses into Cancer again, making favorable aspects to Pisces transits, including Venus. This promises enthusiasm and brings motivation. As winter wanes social prospects are bright and you can accomplish much with ease. This heightened vitality adds to your charisma. Charm a rival; enjoy athletic events.

HEALTH
Jupiter, the celestial healer, transits your health sector from the springtime through December 18. This whole nine-month cycle is wonderful for reaching fitness goals. Explore new variations in diet and exercise regimes. It's a time to grow in strength and wellness. Break any counterproductive habits. Healing techniques from other cultures can be worth trying since the sign of Sagittarius is accented at this time.

LOVE
From May 9–June 5 Venus will frolic in your sign while flirting with a trine to Uranus in Pisces. A new love is promised and might surprise you. Mars, the ruler of passion, brings excitement. It passes twice through your sign, from September 29–December 31 and from March 5, 2008 through the winter. Expect intense emotional needs and attractions during those times. A bond can deepen, but listen if a loved one hints that you're too intense or difficult.

SPIRITUALITY
Your 9th house of spirituality is ruled by Neptune and Pisces. A mutual reception involving Uranus is impacting this sector. It's time to explore spiritual traditions. Allow your intuition and inspiration free rein. Some unique realizations can be revealed if you're receptive. Your previously cherished beliefs are shifting and transforming this year. The ninety days before and after the total lunar eclipse on August 28 promise some profound spiritual experiences. Heed synchronicities and omens.

FINANCE
Solemn Saturn has been clamping down on your finances. Economize. On September 3 Saturn changes signs and pressures ease. Business travel and important meetings can provide lucrative opportunities between Mabon and All Hallows. Written affirmations for prosperity can be very helpful now. Prepare them when the Moon is New in Earth signs, on May 16, September 11, and January 8. Read them daily and visualize a bright fountain of riches pouring upon you.

LEO

The year ahead for those
born under the sign of the Lion
July 23–August 22

With the clarity of bright sunlight, this Sun-ruled second fixed sign of fire radiates poise and magnetism. Confidence, dignity, warmth, and affection are associated with Leo. A colorful approach to life gives you an affinity with the entertainment industry. You easily establish a special rapport with the very young.

Business and pleasure combine beautifully during early spring. Venus transits your 10th house of career until mid-April. Make your work environment more beautiful and comfortable. The last half of April is a perfect time for a spiritual journey or to make decisions about continuing education. Writing and study of all kinds will be a success, for Mercury in your sister fire sign of Aries is well aspected in your 9th house. May 1-15 Mars squares Pluto in mutable signs, impacting your 5th and 8th houses. Love enters a volatile phase; a hint of fate, a past life attraction can surround a relationship. A change of heart is in progress. On June 6 Venus enters your sign and forms a fortunate grand trine aspect with planets in the other fire signs. The good times roll on through July 14. Develop new social contacts or build upon an existing relationship. Using your creative gifts could bring added income now.

During the last half of July, Mercury moves rapidly through your sector of dreams and reverie. Through Lammas and into early August it aspects Uranus favorably. Deep meditations help you understand your life's purpose. Research projects of all kinds are successful now. From August 5-19 Mercury joins the Sun in your sign. Follow through when sudden travel opportunities arise. A change of scene stimulates your intellect. Venus is retrograde in Leo during most of August through September 9, promising a second chance at a lost love. An old hobby can be reawakened, bringing much pleasure. In September serious Saturn departs after giving you a reality check for more than two years. A sense of lightness and release prevails.

October finds Mercury turning retrograde in your home and family sector. Contemplate before making changes in living arrangements. A relative can seem confused or unpredictable. All Hallows brings a greeting from an old friend. At the sabbat, bless your residence. On November 2 Mercury goes direct. New options appear, and those closest to you have a better sense of direction. As December approaches Sagittarius, planets, including the Sun, Jupiter, and Pluto, gather in your sector of romance and pleasure. Participate in a classroom environment or tour group. New places and acquaintances usher in a very happy cycle. You'll be appreciated. Take note of imaginative ideas which come to you spontaneously now. One will be a real gem. You have new talents emerging. At Yule Jupiter enters your 6th house which has a link to animal companions. A beloved creature can reveal new vistas of truth and perception.

As January begins a retrograde influence from Saturn impacts your sector of finances. Seek answers to security issues by understanding patterns linked to your work. Your established reputation and contacts with past business associates can provide a foundation enabling you to move forward. The Full Moon in Leo on January 22 highlights your potentials. Your charisma is especially evident from then through Candlemas. Through February 19 retrograde Mercury opposes your Sun while playing tag with Neptune and Chiron in Aquarius. Be a good listener; compromise is the key to coping with others' ideas. Double-check rules and directions. A legal matter may need attention. From late February through mid-March Venus moves rapidly through your sector of partnership. A talented, loving individual expresses admiration. A business or personal commitment can be finalized advantageously. From March 15-20, a quincunx from a stellium of planets in Pisces in your 8th house brings hidden facts to light. A message from the spirit world reminds you of the mysteries of the afterlife. Adapt. Fate will provide for your needs. It's an excellent time to visit an antique store or thrift shop in search of an unexpected treasure.

HEALTH

Saturn, which is linked to time, rules your house of health. Be aware of how your time management impacts your well-being. Transit Saturn remains in Leo until September. Since Saturn relates to bones and teeth, regular dental care and perhaps some calcium supplements can enhance wellness during the spring and summer. Your energy level should improve as autumn nears. At the winter solstice Jupiter enters your health sector. A cycle of better vitality commences.

LOVE

Love can transform you from the vernal equinox through late December, for Jupiter and Pluto hover in your love sector. Allow relationships to widen your perspective. This is a year for exploration and adventure in love. A camping trip could be the perfect way to get to know someone better. Love trends are especially promising from June through early October when Venus retrogrades in and out of your sign.

SPIRITUALITY

Explore various images of The Hermit, Tarot Key 9. Contemplate the deeper messages in this card. Mars, which rules your 9th house of the higher mind, is making a long passage through your 12th house of peace and retreat. This begins in late September and continues through New Year's Eve, then repeats again from March 5 through winter's end. Higher awareness comes from within during your most solitary moments.

FINANCE

Three of this year's four eclipses impact your finances. This relates to new elements affecting income potential. Patience, effort, and flexibility assure financial success now. The September 11 solar eclipse in your 2nd house suggests changing values. You might find your source of income following a new path. Generate some positive feng shui by passing along belongings or supplies you're no longer using.

VIRGO

The year ahead for those
born under the sign of the Virgin
August 23-September 22

Those born under this second mutable and second of the earth signs dwell upon perfection. Ruled by clever Mercury, Virgo is the alchemist. You refine raw materials, combining intellect with craftsmanship. Cleanliness, service, and health are values sacred to the Virgin.

A zest for adventure overcomes you at the vernal equinox. Mercury is in opposition in early spring, while it squares both Jupiter and Pluto. Enjoy a gamble, but only risk that which you can afford to lose. From mid-April through Beltane, Venus crosses your midheaven, brightening your sector of fame and fortune. Recognition comes, and a friend gives your career a boost. Competitive elements are present during mid-May. A Mars opposition makes others a little difficult. Be diplomatic and independent. Accept help if it is offered, but don't make any demands. As May concludes, Mercury begins a passage through your 11th house, creating a favorable sextile aspect to your Sun through August 4. Become involved in organizations. You can forge some worthwhile friendships. Mercury is retrograde near Midsummer's Day. A companion from the past might resurface. If summer travel plans are discussed in late June or early July, choose to return to an old haunt instead of exploring new territory.

From July 15–August 8 Venus hovers on the cusp of your sign as it goes retrograde. Enjoy the present with companions, but reflect before making a commitment. A past life regression near the Full Moon of July 29 is very healing for heartache or chronic health conditions. Lammas has an energetic quality, as Mars trines your Sun through August 7. During mid-August your 12th house is accented. Quietly performing anonymous acts of kindness brings you a deep happiness, and you might unknowingly befriend an angel in disguise. From August 20–September 5 Mercury moves rapidly through your sign aspecting several mutable sign planets, including Jupiter and Pluto. Select priorities; prepare to take on a new project or make a journey. Saturn begins a two-year transit through your sign near your birthday. A serious, businesslike phase commences. Contentment is found if you become enmeshed in worthwhile work and prepare for the future. The Virgo eclipse at the New Moon on September 11 brings the specifics into focus. Establish a connection with the Earth at the autumn equinox. October finds Venus brightening your sign through November 8. Accept and issue invitations.

November brings Libra transits into your 2nd house. Assemble information, ask questions; there might be a new source of income available. From early December until Yule your 4th house is accented. Family life is a focus; do all that you can to make your home cheerful and comfortable. On the solstice Saturn turns retrograde, a trend that continues through the entire winter season. Pressures ease. The universe offers you a second chance to overcome an obstacle or to take a breather. Jupiter enters Capricorn for a yearlong stay at the same time, creating a harmonious aspect in your 5th house of love and pleasure. January finds you enjoying promising romantic prospects. There's more time for recreation. If you have a yen to become more involved in art or music, now is the time to do so.

At the end of January, Pluto begins a rare sign change and brushes the cusp of Capricorn. Your feelings about children may intensify. You'll become more aware of what a potent force true love really is. At Candlemas Mars changes direction in your 10th house. An authority figure leaves your career environment. Your ambitions are rekindled. The eclipses in February introduce new trends in alternative health. An emotional release is due. Early March finds Neptune joined by other Aquarius transits in your 6th house. Examine ways to get organized. Intuition combined with intellect makes you a star. The last week of winter Mercury, Venus, and the Sun are in a wide conjunction with Uranus in Pisces, your opposing sign. Other people make plans and decisions involving you. Cooperate.

HEALTH
Release all that is stale and counterproductive. It's a wonderful time to overcome habits. Try new health care regimes at the February 6 eclipse in Aquarius. Your house of health is ruled by Uranus, which is in an ongoing mutual reception with Neptune. This favors overcoming chronic conditions.

However, Uranus opposes your Sun. Be aware of how associates affect your health. If someone frustrates or drains you, keep your distance. There could be a psychic vampire hovering nearby.

LOVE
The retrograde Venus transit of July 28–September 9 impacts your 1st and 12th houses. A deeper understanding of what your needs are as well as what you can offer a companion develops at that time. If a relationship isn't working, face up to the facts at Lammas and perform a ritual of release. Your love sector is doubly blessed by both Jupiter and Pluto when they begin long transits through Capricorn during the winter season.

SPIRITUALITY
Saturn enters your sign near your birthday this year. Suitable and satisfying work awakens your spiritual side. Earth sign energies are always connected to spiritual growth for you because Taurus rules your 9th house. Enlist the help of earth elementals. Meditate on the bark of a twisted tree and hold a favorite stone when the Moon is in an earth sign to seek a closer connection.

FINANCE
Libra is on the cusp of your 2nd house of finances. Developing a balanced budget is your first step toward assuring security. Work to clear away old debts before early September when Saturn enters your sign. Then you can begin to establish a secure foundation for the long-term future. The winter months usher in a series of favorable aspects to your Sun. This should bring you progress.

LIBRA

The year ahead for those
born under the sign of the Scales
September 23–October 23

Seeking love, understanding, and harmony is the quest of Libra, the second of the air signs and the third cardinal sign. A yen for tranquillity and a desire to look at all sides of an argument make you hesitant to take sides in a confrontation.

Companions make your life quite exciting during the early days of spring. Mars in your 5th house of pleasure opposes Saturn through April 5. Neptune's presence in this aspect pattern lends a note of glamorous confusion to social situations. Trust your intuition; situations begin to clarify under the Full Moon in Libra on April 2. During the second week of April, Jupiter turns retrograde in your 3rd house, a pattern in effect until early August. It's a wonderful cycle for strengthening relationships with neighbors or siblings. Mid-April through May 8 Venus in your sister air sign of Gemini forms a series of favorable aspects, including a trine to Neptune. Love connections abound. Travel is especially enjoyable. Mid-May through Midsummer's Day finds Mars in Aries, your opposing sign. Approach difficult people with tolerance.

Throughout June, July, and early August, Mercury makes a long passage through your 10th house. There is much to learn regarding your profession.

Study and conversations provide useful insights. At Lammastide contemplate available career choices. It's time to make decisions and commit. Venus, your ruler, is retrograde throughout August and early September in your 11th and 12th houses. Expressing your deepest feelings can feel awkward. Maintain a lighthearted approach to relationships. A new perspective concerning a love connection from the past brings peace and acceptance. The eclipses on August 28 and September 11 emphasize health care and service to those less fortunate. You'll have the chance to return a favor. Dreams offer valuable guidance.

Near the autumn equinox, Mercury in Libra forms a grand trine in air signs with Mars in Gemini and Neptune in Aquarius. Your insight is keen. Begin new projects from September 19 until the eve of the Harvest Moon on the 26th. The stars spell success for you as your birthday nears. October begins with Mars moving into your career sector where it remains through December. You'll have an urge to seek a promotion. Consider redecorating your workspace. At Samhain offer a blessing on your place of employment to clear away residual tension. At the end of October through November 11 Mercury completes a retrograde pattern in your sign. A problem is solved.

The remainder of November brings wonderful social opportunities, as Venus in Libra conjoins your Sun in the 1st house. Your charm opens new doors, both in your professional and personal life. The week of the Gemini Full Moon on November 24 favors networking. Answer all letters and calls in early December. A stellium of Sagittarius planets impacts your 3rd house, promising a variety of activities and the presentation of interesting ideas. At the winter solstice Jupiter begins a yearlong passage in your home and family sector. Overall, your living arrangements are improving. Create a talisman of mistletoe at Yule and hang it yearlong to preserve protective forces gathering now. During January Mars retrogrades back into Gemini. The teacher and the crusader within you emerges.

By Candlemas Pluto brushes your 4th house cusp as it begins a rare sign change. There is much to learn about your heritage. February accents your sector of pleasure and romance with several Aquarius transits, including Mercury and Venus favorably aspecting your Sun. The eclipse on February 6 favors pursuing a new avocation. Be creative. Winter's last days find cardinal sign transits from Mars and Jupiter creating strong aspects on the angles of your birth chart. Live in the present; expect a very dynamic time. Strategy helps you balance career demands with home life. Careful scheduling is the key to making everything work out smoothly.

HEALTH

The eclipse pattern this year links directly to your health. Be aware of changes in your vitality and new factors impacting wellness at the end of August. The role of caregiver may come your way as the year ends. Caring for a dear one can be fulfilling, but don't let it tire you. Reasonable precautions to guard your own wellbeing are a must. A very clean and organized environment can do wonders for your health now.

LOVE

The Venus retrograde from July 28–September 9 promises a new understanding of lost loves that just weren't meant to be. A reunion at that time can be very healing. You are the quintessential romantic. April, November, and February favor exploring tender passions. Serve French or Chinese cuisine by candlelight to one whom you would woo during those times. Light the way for Cupid's arrows with a pair of rose-colored candles.

SPIRITUALITY

May, August, September, January, and February are all cycles when your 9th house of spirituality is activated by Gemini transits. These are ideal times to learn about other faiths. Share ideas and listen carefully. Try a Sanskrit mantra or draw a colorful mandala to express your thoughts regarding spiritual growth. Carl Jung's writings about mandalas in therapy could be helpful. Examine his work in order to acquire deeper insights.

FINANCE

The fixed signs of Scorpio and Taurus rule your finances. Examine habits regarding money management. Figure out what hasn't been working and don't repeat the pattern. The early spring is wonderful for reviewing insurance coverage, investments, and tax strategies. The winter holidays usher in an upbeat Venus tie, enabling you to increase your earning ability. Be alert. Follow through with a promising opportunity near Yuletide. Friends offer valuable insights to help you discover new sources of income near the winter solstice.

SCORPIO

The year ahead for those
born under the sign of the Scorpion
October 24–November 21

Driven by a sense of purpose, Scorpio is both intense and subtle. Second of the water signs and third among the fixed signs, Scorpio has a traditional association with all that is mysterious. Others are not easily admitted to the innermost sanctum of your being. Your trust must be cultivated respectfully first.

The early days of spring find retrograde Saturn in fiery Leo powerfully aspected by other fixed sign transits. Your 10th and 4th houses are involved. Catch up on work-related responsibilities but don't accept new tasks until your home life is balanced. During April various volatile situations gradually resolve. Talented companions stimulate your creative side from March 20–April 11 when Venus is in your partnership sector. A loved one needs more of your time. During mid-April through May 15 Mars in Pisces pleasantly blesses you with added vitality. Let the Full Moon in Scorpio on May 2 shine on your pillow. A dream stimulated by a Beltane ritual could bring you guidance.

During June, Venus joins Saturn in your 10th house of fame and fortune. Your career surroundings will be more pleasant; a friend offers you encouragement and opportunity. Socialize with professional associates near the summer solstice. Independence Day finds Mercury retrograde in your 9th house of travel. Take a sentimental journey to a childhood home or to invite old friends to your residence for a Fourth of July reunion. On July 10, when Mercury changes direction, one of the best travel cycles all year commences. This trend remains in force through August 4. A cruise or overseas journey would be very successful. Keep a travel journal, send post cards. At Lammastide make the celebration bright and light. A grouping of fire sign transits in Leo and Sagittarius impacts your 2nd and 10th houses throughout the remainder of August. Be alert to novel income opportunities. The August 28 eclipse in Pisces promises changes of heart in the weeks ahead. You can fall in and out of love quickly during the last days of summer. A creative idea is worth exploring then too.

On September 2 Saturn changes signs, commencing a two-and-a-half-year passage through your 11th house. Pluto, your ruler, goes direct on September 8. Friends are about to become more serious and enlist your help in community projects or charities. Mabon finds you concerned about choosing worthwhile goals. The first three weeks of October, Mercury is in your sign where it turns retrograde on October 12. Be thoughtful about communication of all kinds. Your words are powerful and will shape your future. Get organized and make reservations if you are traveling. Your destination may change midcourse, but a journey should still be successful. At All Hallows a favorable Sun-Mars aspect in water signs favors connecting with dolphin spirits, undines, and mermaids. Trust your emotions and intuition now.

During the last half of November Mercury enters Scorpio again. Your state of mind will be positive. Relationships between grandparent and grandchild are excellent near Thanksgiving. In December Venus enters Scorpio where it remains for most of the month. Yuletide presents happy social connections. January brings promise and freshness as Pluto, ruler of Scorpio, brushes the Sagittarius-Capricorn cusp. Your 3rd house is a focus. Your neighborhood is holding secrets; learn more about its history. A deeper understanding of sibling relationships brings peace to childhood recollections. Candlemas finds Mercury retrograde in your home and family sector. Conversations with relatives are helpful. Lost items can reappear mysteriously. The February eclipse pattern could promise a move or introduce a new relative into the household. Winter ends with Venus bowing into your love and pleasure sector. Pursue romance, make time to do what you enjoy most in March. The fine arts can add dimension to your life.

HEALTH

With Mars linked to your health sector, Scorpio's survival skills are legendary. Often those born under this sign will completely bounce back from life-threatening situations. When Mars is retrograde November 16–January 31 the health consequences of past choices become apparent. Conquer any dietary or lifestyle factors which undermine your wellbeing. Include basil in Candlemas celebrations to honor your newfound strength.

LOVE

Three of this year's eclipses strongly aspect Uranus in your love sector, by either conjunction or opposition. Love and friendship have an interchangeable quality. Support changes loved ones want to make. Wait until after the August 28 eclipse passes to make a change in your partnership status. Your heart's desire can assume a new aspect near that date. Dedicate a burgundy candle with vanilla oil. Light it as you wish to discover true love.

SPIRITUALITY

The active pursuit of spiritual awakening is likely from August 8 through March. Mars transits in Cancer and Gemini make a long passage through your sectors of philosophy, the higher mind, and the spirit world. A pilgrimage to a spiritual site or a past life regression then would enhance enlightenment. Consider attending a séance between Samhain and the winter solstice. It could bring you deep peace and comfort concerning the afterlife and guidance from those who have passed.

FINANCE

Pluto is starting to exit your 2nd house where it has been for many years. A less intense attitude toward finances surfaces. Financial goals can be attained from spring through mid-December, for benevolent Jupiter blesses your sector of income then. Jupiter aspects Saturn in Leo favorably from the vernal equinox through August. That's a good time to seek financial advice and apply for loans and grants. Iron pyrite is a wonderful prosperity stone to carry or keep in your workplace.

SAGITTARIUS
The year ahead for those
born under the sign of the Archer
November 22–December 21

Optimistic, adventurous, and outspoken, Sagittarius is the third sign of both the fire and mutable categories. As a restless idealist, new horizons forever beckon you. You will not tolerate boundaries or restrictions in your quest for truth.

Spring begins on a note of ease and plenty. Benevolent Jupiter, your ruler, is in your sign, exactly trining Saturn in Leo. Through mid-May others are helpful. Opportunities for wish fulfillment are yours for the asking. On April 11 Mercury begins a rapid transit through your sector of romance and pleasure. Travel can facilitate love. A talkative, intelligent companion brings happiness. Early May finds Venus in opposition to your Sun. Expect opposing views about a relationship. Allow others to do as they wish. On May 16 dynamic Mars enters Aries, giving you wonderful motivation. The Full Moon in your sign on May 31 puts you in touch with your goals. Through Midsummer's Day you'll accomplish much. This trend also favors exercise programs.

Your 8th house is accented during July with transits in Cancer. It's a perfect time to catch up on any neglected financial obligations. A mystery is solved near July 10 when Mercury changes direction. A message of inspiration arrives from the spirit world, encoded in an unexpected story, song, or joke. At Lammastide appreciate and honor the past. On August 7 Jupiter completes its retrograde, turning direct in conjunction with your Sun. Widen your horizons and move forward. Venus makes a very well aspected trine in your 9th house August 9–October 8. You would enjoy a program of higher education or spiritual studies. New friendships with foreign-born people are likely to develop. Eclipses in August and September point to sudden changes in career aspirations or residence. Pluto also completes its retrograde in your 1st house. You might want to move to a home which is easier to care for or more comfortable. At Mabon perform a blessing on your surroundings.

During October your 11th and 12th houses are accented. Spend time in tranquil contemplation. Mid-October brings you deep personal joy through helping needy animals or disadvantaged people. At All Hallows an office party adds a happy social note to the sabbat festivities. November 1-11 finds Mercury turning direct in Libra while making positive aspects to both Neptune and Jupiter. Your ability to communicate is in top form. Trust a hunch. Late November through early December brings a sextile from Venus in your sector of wishes and social contacts. It's an optimum time for networking. Respond enthusiastically to offers of friendship. On December 2 Mercury joins the Sun and Pluto in your 1st house. Travel plans are likely; your ideas impact others. Cultivate your image. Reputation is a sensitive issue. For Yule, try a new hairstyle or wardrobe items. New Year's

Eve finds Venus brightening your sign where it will remain until January 24. One of the best cycles for romance, creativity, and overall change for the better commences. At the same time, though, Mars retrogrades back into Gemini, your opposing sign. Avoid confrontation. Keep your competitive spirit in check. At the end of January, Pluto exits your sign. You'll feel less tense than you have in many years. At Candlemas a deep meditation helps you to understand your new priorities.

The February 6 eclipse highlights your 3rd house. You'll be on the go. A new vehicle might be needed, but wait until February 19 to select one. The lunar eclipse on February 20 emphasizes balancing career goals with family life. Since Uranus is prominent, be flexible. An unexpected turn of events is likely before the month's end. March brings a potent emphasis on water sign planets. Be patient if someone close to you is moody and sensitive. On March 12 benevolent, loving Venus enters your home and family sector where it remains through the end of winter. It's easier to keep relatives happy and to relax at home. A visitor proves to be good company. Be hospitable.

HEALTH

Pluto's sign change, which begins in January, augurs a shift toward alternative healthcare. The application of heated stones or compresses to your abdomen, back, and legs might be very helpful. With Scorpio ruling your health sector, past life regression could also help you to attune to your body's needs. Mysterious health conditions can have a karmic cause.

LOVE

With impatient, assertive Mars ruling your 5th house of romance, you enjoy a challenge. You do tend to live in the moment. Regarding close relationships, don't ever rush a situation. Venus' placement from June through October is extraordinarily promising for romance. An established tie can move to a new dimension of intimacy or a new liaison can develop. Travel might play a role in this. Finalize decisions about your commitment status after Venus completes its retrograde on September 9.

SPIRITUALITY

Serious Saturn completes a two-year passage through your 9th house late in the summer. You've been exploring different beliefs and may have been disappointed by a certain guru or coven. Accepting this philosophically will bring you peace by Mabon. Your greatest spiritual lessons this year come through personal exploration and journeys. These increase near your birthday when Jupiter and Pluto conjoin in your sign.

FINANCE

Others impact your finances this year, for Mars makes a long passage through Cancer, your 8th house of shared assets. Be alert concerning the ways partners manage joint resources. A legacy can be received or an investment might prove to be profitable. Don't be tempted by any kind of financial risk now. Insurance coverage can be a source of concern. If so, explore new options. From early spring until December 19 Jupiter is in your sign, greatly favoring overall growth and success.

CAPRICORN

The year ahead for those
born under the sign of the Goat
December 22–January 19

Saturn, the celestial timekeeper, rules this third earth sign and fourth cardinal sign. Capricorns tend to have a rather difficult early life. However, their later years often are truly golden. Saturn has always favored the not so very youthful. Ambitious and practical, you instinctively know how to consolidate.

Early spring is awash with romance. Ostara finds Venus in Taurus, happily aspecting your love and pleasure sector. You are popular and appreciated. By mid-April you might even have to choose between several prospects. Near All Fool's Day the stars favor cultural pursuits. Saturn completes its retrograde in your 8th house before May Day. Dedicate a Beltane ritual to release, renewal, and exploring the mysteries of the afterlife. End mourning of any kind at the sabbat rite. The first half of May promises intense conversations, for Mars is sextile your Sun from the 3rd house. Discuss problems, but don't argue. Then progress is assured. Venus opposes you from the 7th house of relationships from May 8–June 5. An attractive person catches your eye. Legal matters are resolved successfully now. During June the focus is on home and family life. Mars creates a stir in the 4th house. A residence might need repair, or you can consider a move. Family members need a great deal of attention. At the summer solstice bless a talisman to protect your household. A healing circle is beneficial to a loved one. The Full Moon on June 30 in your sign brings a culmination. You'll feel confident selecting priorities and releasing old projects.

July finds Mercury midway through a long passage in Cancer. Stimulating companions have much to teach you. Listen to alternative plans and ideas. On July 14 Venus enters Virgo and creates harmonious patterns in your 9th house. A marvelous cycle for summer travel commences. Expect heightened physical vitality near Lammas. Mars is strong then, a trend lasting until August 7. Approach all challenges with confidence. Go after what you truly desire. August 20–September 5 brings a trine from Mercury in your 9th house. Your mind is sharp and your words eloquent. The lunar eclipse on August 28 can bring an interesting situation with a neighbor or sibling into a new light.

The autumn equinox is all about career for you. The Sun and Mercury highlight your sector of aspiration and recognition, the 10th house. You'll be more visible professionally and might take on added responsibilities. October marks a very dynamic cycle. Mars makes a series of powerful cardinal sign aspects. Partnership and possibly legal matters can be involved. Avoid confrontational people. Employ subtle strategy if arguments develop. Keep strong competitive urges on an ethical level. On October 9 Venus returns to a favorable angle in your 9th house where it remains through November 8. Friendships can develop through study groups or spiritual circles. November and early December bring recognition linked to your career. Venus is strongly aspected in your 10th house. A friend's good will and kind recommendation open a door for you. Attend all office social functions near Thanksgiving. Jupiter commences a yearlong passage through your sign on December 19. Well deserved rewards from past efforts arrive. As your birthday nears, life is bright with the promise of better times ahead. A retrograde Mars in your relationship sector at Yuletide hints that a past partnership might be revived. Be aware of patterns. Good or not, an associate is about to repeat them. At the Full Moon on December 23 this situation peaks. Consult your extended family about a significant relationship. Follow advice.

Mutable sign planets aspect retrograde Saturn in early January. Focus on health. Release stress, prepare wholesome meals. There is so much going on that you can feel overwhelmed. From January 25–February 17 Venus brightens your sign. A very happy social cycle commences. Wrap a small, thoughtful gift for your loved one at Candlemas. Your workload lightens and it's easier to enjoy simple pleasures. March opens with Mars in Cancer moving into an opposition with Pluto in your sign. Throughout the rest of winter you'll have a new awareness of how others impact your life. Choose associates with great care. A sense of changing times ahead prevails. Be progressive.

HEALTH

Mars moves in and out of your 6th house of health in August–September and again during January–February. Be aware of recurring health conditions then. It's also a time to be gentle with yourself while breaking any negative health habits. Apache tears and the onyx are gems to carry for health.

LOVE

Long-term, life-changing transits are aspecting your 5th house of love through the other earth signs. Beginning with Saturn's entry into Virgo in September, followed by Jupiter and Pluto moving into Capricorn in December and January, respectively, your attitude toward love and capacity for developing a deep, meaningful relationship undergoes profound transformation. Focus on growth and all will be well.

SPIRITUALITY

The eclipse of September 11 falls in your 9th house of philosophy and spirituality. The late summer and early autumn emphasize spiritual awakening. Since Saturn is strong, a very ancient spiritual tradition would prove valuable. Establishing deeper mystical connections with small animal companions can be very healing and rewarding.

FINANCE

A Neptune–Saturn opposition affects your financial sectors through August. Your own intuition provides the best guidance. You're growing more idealistic about monetary matters. The mutual reception involving Neptune and Uranus reveals that exercising originality can add to your earning powers. The eclipse of February 6 falls in your 2nd house, indicating that cash can be earned in a new way at winter's end. Be progressive and flexible, then all will be well.

AQUARIUS

The year ahead for those
born under the sign of the Water Bearer
January 20–February 18

Ruled by the zodiac's magician, Uranus, Aquarius is the fourth fixed sign and the third of the air signs. Inventive, independent, original, and a friend to all, you are a progressive reformer.

Spring fever prevails from the vernal equinox through April 5 as Mars conjoins Neptune in your sign. You're restless but have tremendous energy. Focus and you'll accomplish a great deal. By mid-April Venus enters Gemini, ruler of your love and pleasure sector. An idyllic romance is likely. The good times roll on through the first week of May. Your artistic ability is in top form. Focus on creative expression. Mid-May finds Mercury trine your Sun. Plan a vacation, work on a writing project or studies. Your mental energy is at a peak. Mars highlights home and family life from June 25–August 7. You're ready to get the house in shape. Take needed safety precautions and ask for help with improvements that may need to be made. Humor or a quiet word is the best response if someone has a fit of temper.

On July 29 the Full Moon falls in your sign. You'll realize how much others admire you and look to you for leadership. At the same time, you'll long to have more freedom from responsibility. Take time for solitary reflection at Lammastide. On August 9 retrograde Venus in Leo steps backward into your 7th house and remains there through the first week of October. An old flame can rekindle. Be aware of patterns in partnerships of all kinds. A deeper quality of love enriches a significant relationship. Wait until after September 9 when Venus changes direction to make any permanent changes in your status. You are exploring intimacy and commitment on a new level. You could change your mind. Near the autumn equinox a grand trine in air signs forms, with Mercury, Mars, and Neptune in aspect. You'll be interested in justice and humanitarian concerns. Your efforts to implement changes of all kinds in your life are rewarded.

From mid-October through November 8 Venus joins Saturn in your 8th house. Financial matters are on your mind. This sector also relates to contact with the afterlife. At Samhain a séance would be a fabulous success. During November Mercury moves rapidly through your career sector, where it conjoins the Sun. At the same time Venus moves into an exceptionally favorable 9th house aspect. It's a wonderful time to seek a promotion or enroll in a program of higher education. The mood grows futuristic as autumn deepens into early winter. Travel for business or study is successful. During the first week of December Jupiter conjoins Pluto in your 11th house. Your social circle widens. Involvement in an organization brings new goals. Your perception of future plans is shifting. As the winter solstice nears, you grow more introspective and enjoy looking inward. Your 12th house is accented from late December through January 7. The power found in silence and the healing qualities of peace and privacy will be cherished throughout the holidays.

On January 8 Mercury begins a long passage through Aquarius. This lasts until March 14 and sets the tone for the winter season. You'll have numerous projects to complete. On February 6 the solar eclipse in your sign augurs surprises. A move at work or home can manifest suddenly. The status quo is disrupted. Adapt. Release that which is no longer a steady factor in your life. The total lunar eclipse on February 20 falls in your 8th house. Someone near you may be considering a new financial track. Tax and insurance matters need attention. The 8th house also relates to the afterlife. An unexpected communication from the other side reinforces your belief in the spirit world. Winter's last days place an emphasis on security. Appreciate all that you have rather than lamenting lack.

HEALTH

Your 6th house of health is highlighted by long transits from both Mercury and Mars this year. Mercury remains there from May 29–August 4. Learning about health will be important. The mind-body connection will be especially apparent during this time. Mars retrogrades in and out of your health sector from September 29–December 31 and again from March 5 through winter's end. Study your health history. Moderate exercise is favored, but do pamper and be gentle with your body. Get extra rest and avoid temperature extremes.

LOVE

Your love sector has a strong link to the sign of Gemini and its ruler, Mercury. The phrase "meeting of the minds" could have been coined to describe your ideal relationship. The local library is a wonderful place for you to socialize. Attend any programs offered there; lectures, readings. book sales. You'll have an enjoyable time and could well meet worthwhile prospects while Cupid hovers. Near May Eve and from mid-November through early December the cosmos favors love. Circulate in pleasant ways and reach out then.

SPIRITUALITY

Pluto and Jupiter both enter your 12th house during the winter season. Time spent alone, either in nature or at a spiritual retreat, enhances your spiritual growth. Heed that small, still voice within. Dreams will be rich with meaning this year, especially near the Full Moon just before Lammas. Remember, a dream uninterpreted is like a letter unread. Don't dismiss a dream lightly, seek to understand its message instead.

FINANCE

Three of this year's eclipses impact your 2nd and 8th houses, both of which link to monetary matters. The keynote of any eclipse is always change. Shifts in the worldwide economic pattern can impact your personal finances. Flexibility and a progressive attitude help you to acquire the security required. With Saturn entering the area affected by joint finances in September, it's important to be aware of how the financial decisions of another might be affecting you. Perform a prosperity ritual at the February Full Moon.

PISCES

The year ahead for those
born under the sign of the Fish
February 19–March 20

There is a haunting, otherworldly atmosphere blurring this fourth of the mutable and third of the water signs. Ruled by elusive Neptune, your world is a subtle one. Receptive and very emotional, changeable and sympathetic, you often feel tugged in different directions by both external conflict and inner turmoil.

Mercury combines with Uranus in your sign during spring's earliest days, delivering excitement. New ideas are discussed, your mental energy is high. The vernal equinox represents exploration, a trend lasting through April 10. Mars brings you energy as it moves through Pisces from early April until May 15. Confrontations are brewing; you're more assertive than usual. From the second week of May until June 5 Venus moves through Cancer, the guardian of your love sector. This is one of the best social cycles of the year. Cultivate romance, pursue a creative project. During the second and third weeks of June cardinal sign transits generate tension in your financial sector. Don't take any risks with security.

July finds Mercury favorably aspecting Mars in water and earth signs. Answers to security-related problems come from a neighbor or loved one. You'll feel more confident after July 10 when Mercury turns direct. Consider taking a cruise or visiting an island at the end of the month. Just before Lammas Venus begins a retrograde. Your 6th and 7th houses are impacted through early September. Old habits affect both health and close partnerships. Repeat only what has traditionally worked well for you. Expect a time of endings and beginnings near the Pisces eclipse of August 28. Your home may require maintenance during September. Mars moves into your home and family sector and will both oppose and square other mutable sign transits. A relocation could be due or a family member or tenant could want to move.

October 1-23 brings a very well aspected grand trine in water signs involving Mercury, Mars, and Uranus. This is wonderful for study, writing, and pursuing the arts. Because of Mercury retrograde, travel to new destinations before October 12, then backtrack along a familiar path later in the month. All Hallows finds much afoot in the life of a close partner, for both Venus and Saturn highlight the 7th house. Select meaningful career goals during November. Sagittarius transits accent your 10th house in a dynamic way, making you more visible to influential professional contacts. Past efforts are rewarded with success near Yuletide. During January a stellium of Capricorn placements including the Sun, Jupiter, Mercury, and, by the month's end, Pluto, affect your 11th house. Attend meetings and social events. It's a great time to seek advice and to network. Prepare a house blessing at Candlemas, for Mars impacts residence and family life. Seek ways to make the house more comfortable.

February's eclipses encourage you to help those in need. Charity projects can change your life near the 7th when your 12th house is highlighted. On the 20th a Virgo eclipse in opposition to you makes you realize the need for cooperation. Attend to legal matters as the month ends. Early March finds you seeking solitude. Avoid crowds until after the New Moon in Pisces on the 7th. The rest of the winter will be quite exciting, with much activity in your 1st house. Purchase new wardrobe items with birthday money. Image and appearance are important. Your social life will be very happy due to strong Venus aspects starting on March 13. Pursue travel opportunities in mid to late March. It's a perfect time to plan a pilgrimage to an area linked to spiritual energies or to investigate a haunted house.

HEALTH

The last few years have found your energy level low and your health has been a concern. That changes when Saturn leaves your 6th house of health in September. Efforts you've made to enhance your wellness start to pay off. When Jupiter enters Capricorn in December it makes a favorable aspect to your Sun. Together they facilitate wellbeing by winter's end. The feet affect your overall health. Invest in a foot reflexology session. The benefits might prove to be truly astounding.

LOVE

There are two time periods this year when your 5th house of love and pleasure is especially active. The first is May 29–August 4 when Mercury is in Cancer. The second involves Mars, the planet of desire and passion. It moves through Cancer September 29–December 31, then returns again from March 5 to the year's end. This points to a very active year for romance. Prepare to discover true love at work, in a school setting, or while traveling. Collect a variety of beautiful seashells and place them in a decorative dish on your altar to attract forces of true love.

SPIRITUALITY

Pluto rules Scorpio, your 9th house of philosophy and spirituality. Pluto is conjunct the galactic center in late Sagittarius for much of the year, accenting spirituality as a priority. In January Pluto begins a rare sign change as it moves into Capricorn. Earthy, natural energies are spiritual catalysts for you. Animals, crystals and live plants can awaken spiritual connections. You'll seek a more tangible expression of spirituality. Meditations and affirmations which address coping with daily life situations appeal to you during this time.

FINANCE

Don't allow a needy companion to drain your resources. Saturn begins an opposition pattern in September which could make you a soft touch. Offer words of encouragement, not cash. Maximize financial opportunities during August, when your 2nd house benefits from especially favorable aspects involving Jupiter and Venus. When Mars is retrograde November 16–January 31 be aware of spending and saving patterns. Learn from past experiences. Settle debts. A lodestone in a green velvet bag is an excellent prosperity talisman for enhancing your financial situation.

GYPSIES

"Gypsy, one scattered race, like stars in the sight of God."

GYPSIES EVOKE images of freedom, bright colors, wild music and dancing, the allure of being "away with the raggle taggle gypsies-o," an apt description of a people with neither written language nor written history. Gypsies are known to themselves as Roma, although the term "gypsy" comes from the incorrect assumption that they originated in Egypt. In fact the first such wanderers came from northwestern India and today about 15 million gypsies can be found in virtually every country. In 1933 a flag was created to unite the Roma worldwide. It was designed with blue on the top half symbolizing the sky and God, and green on the bottom half, representing a connection to the Earth Mother. In 1971 an additional symbol, a red 16-spoke chakra wheel was included in the center of the flag to identify the Roma as originating in India.

The Romanis abide by numerous disciplines, with rules and rituals governing everything, including dying and death. In an attempt to keep Death at bay from the dying, complicated measures are taken to create distractions. Gypsies shout, clap, change the name of the patient, or attempt transferring the malady to an object or animal – all in hope of sending Death off on a false trail. If Death does manage to capture its quarry, the effort shifts toward keeping evil spirits away from the body on its way to burial. Mourners scatter kernels of corn at intersections or any area with the shape of a cross. There is much wailing in grief. When a person dies, their clothing isn't given to family members or neighbors – wearing someone else's clothes is forbidden. The garments of the dead must be burned so the spirits can be released.

Most gypsy folk tales exemplify the aspects of life they consider most important – enough food, a place to sleep, beautiful music and love. The Czech story, "The Rom in the Piano," touches on all these points, as well as the gypsy fondness for the violin and a bit of trickery. The protagonist receives a magic violin from God which causes the listener to dance continuously, unable to stop until the music ceases. A princess, enchanted by the playing, thinks it comes from a special piano in her bedroom where the Rom is hiding. At night he sneaks out, helps himself to leftover feast, sleeps with the princess, and the next morning slips back into the piano to resume playing for visiting kings. The kings all want to own the magical instrument. They are amazed when the Rom leaps out of the piano, claims he was hiding inside, and the beautiful music was in fact played by a violin. The monarchs then proceed to hire gypsy violinists for their own kingdoms. Now, since the Rom has accomplished his purpose, he leaves the princess and returns to his wife and family.

For him, life is for the moment, to enjoy with no looking back and no regrets. Gypsy music also embodies the essence of what it means to have no roots, singing about love, heartache, and wandering without regard for a sense of history or belonging. Many gypsies are unaware of the huge numbers that were tortured or put to death by the Nazis during the Holocaust. Some governments are trying to effect a change by requiring Roma children to attend school where they happen to alight. Certain English towns, for instance, have designated areas for the travelers to set up temporary camp. In some countries gypsies have succumbed to the pressures of modern politics and have removed the wheels from their caravans, creating a "permanent" encampment. But whether wandering the world or traveling only in their hearts, the Roma people always abide with zest and passion.

– LAURA CONLEY

☀ the fixed stars

NASHIRA – THE FORTUNATE ONE. Long ago, as the first horoscopes were being drawn, ancient astrologers divided the celestial bodies into three groups. There were the luminaries, the "bright lights," the Sun and Moon. The stars that moved rapidly were called "planets," from a word which means "wanderer." The last group, by far the most numerous, are the fixed stars. There are many thousands of them. Each one glittering in the night sky is a Sun, glowing by generating its own light. Many may be surrounded by a solar system of planets like our own. Variations in distance and chemical composition give the fixed stars different colors and magnitude, or brightness. Astrologically this means that each creates unique cosmic energies, some positive and some sinister. The term "fixed" is rather a misnomer. The stars do move, but very, very slowly. Astrologers took a long time to recognize this movement because the distance covered in a century is barely perceptible.

Nashira is a star whose name means "She Who Brings Good News," or "The Fortunate One" in Arabic. Currently located at 20 degrees of Aquarius, 33 minutes 52 seconds, Nashira is truly a lucky star. The legendary astrologer Ptolemy related the nature of Nashira to that of the benevolent, generous planet Jupiter stabilized by Saturn. When active in the horoscope of a person or in an event chart, Nashira's presence turns hardship to success. Evil is overcome by goodness. Success in government matters as well as a gift for writing come to light when Nashira shines. However caution prevails regarding wild or large animals. Especially at this time they must be handled with thought and skill or injury tends to occur.

Those born from February 8 to 14 have Nashira conjunct the Sun. Many important and powerful individuals, including Abraham Lincoln and Charles Darwin, were born during this time. However Nashira impacts other birthdates as well. Check your horoscope for planets positioned from 19 to 25 degrees of Aquarius. These are within orb of being positively affected by this angel among the stars. According to the nature of the planet in question and its house position, Nashira will stimulate a realization of its highest and best potentials.

From spring 2007 through early 2008, Neptune will transit from 20 to 22 degrees of Aquarius, in exact conjunction with Nashira. Neptune relates to all that is fanciful and illusionary as well as beautiful, including elves and fairies. Overall spiritual awakening can be expected. Those who meditate and study yoga can make great progress. Mediumship, tarot and other esoteric subjects can provide new levels of enlightenment. The fine arts, especially music and dance, will be favorably affected. New types of music and dance forms can emerge. Neptune in Aquarius is in mutual reception with Uranus in Pisces. This cosmic shape shift brings a Uranian element to Nashira's message. New technologies are perfected to solve old problems.

Remembering the ancient caution this star gives regarding animals, it's important to note that Neptune rules marine life. Swimmers, divers, fishermen and sailors would be wise to respect the ecology of the sea and to exercise caution when they encounter the creatures of the deep.

From March 24 to 30, 2007, Mars will transit in conjunction with Nashira. This time period favors athletes and all kinds of adventurous undertakings. Military matters will take a fortunate turn. Those who handle animals must use special caution, especially advisable at competitive events such as dog shows and horse shows.

From March 4 to 12, 2008, Mercury and Venus will conjoin Nashira. The release of new works of visual art, films or books is favored. It's a time when writers, students, travelers and artists will all find that their undertakings are blessed.

– Dikki-Jo Mullen

Arabian astronomer constructing a celestial globe, from Alboul Hassan Ali's *Praeclarissimum in Juditijs Astrorum*, Venice, 1519

PYTHAGORAS

Through numbers, magic

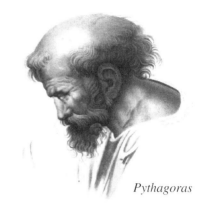

Pythagoras

KNOWLEDGE ABOUT Pythagoras the scientist tends to merge into Pythagoras the myth. He has been termed "The Patron Saint of Science," "The Father of Philosophy," and in odd conjunction, "Son of Apollo." An ancient chronicle assures us that on a day when Pythagoras was out walking, a stream crossed his path. The water raised from its bed and acclaimed, "Hail Pythagoras!" We're not prepared to vouch for the story. But as the father of modern geometry, number theory and music science, the accomplishments of Pythagoras reached mythic proportions.

The Pythian Oracle of Delphi predicted his greatness "to all men throughout all time." Born around 569-590 BC, Pythagoras grew up studying with the priests of Samos. He traveled to Egypt in pursuit of knowledge, and once knocked on a temple door at midnight. No one answered. Pythagoras remained there, attacked by dogs and mocked by slaves, until he was admitted at dawn. But his ordeal didn't end there. The Egyptian priesthood thought little of Greeks and subjected Pythagoras to a dramatic hazing rite. Undeterred, he went from temple to temple until he found one more hospitable.

Pythagoras studied the Egyptian mysteries for twenty-two years. At that point Egypt was invaded, and he was taken with the Egyptian priests to Babylon. He remained there for twelve years, studying the mysteries of the Babylonians, Hebrews, Chaldeans, and by some accounts, Indian Brahmans and Hyperborean Druids. Pythagoras concluded from these experiences that all religions and their gods derived from the same source.

Pythagoras returned to Greece at the age of fifty-six. He set about founding several mystery schools and communities, including the Temple of the Muses and the Order of Pythagoreans. Pythagoras taught his initiates orally, writing only in symbols and secret characters; he did not believe all people were ready for enlightenment. The lectures began with lighting a candle, symbolically keeping away the dark. During his public lectures, Pythagoras hung a curtain and spoke to the uninitiated from "beyond the veil." Only his initiated students were allowed in to view him. Pythagoras taught to "exceed not the balance," meaning to avoid excess in all things and to "stir not the fire with the sword" – to refrain from spreading the truth by force.

His schools had four areas of study: number theory, music, geometry and astronomy. Each day began and ended with a recitation of the Golden Verses. These seventy-one passages reminded the male and female Pythagoreans of the moral values by which they should live.

They included honoring what fate has given, including the gods, nature spirits, heroes and families. The verses went on to stress choosing wisely what fate hadn't decreed but which mortals chose, such as friendships and living habits.

To Pythagoras, the number was sacred. Pythagoreans didn't acknowledge the number zero since all came from a single source, or the number one, and nothing could exist without it. They looked at patterns and ratios in nature to express the laws of the universe. Because fractions did not occur in nature, Pythagoreans didn't acknowledge them as true numbers.

Pythagoras used the magical study of numbers to prove there was order to the universe. He believed that everything in the world operated in divine harmony with the laws of nature. Pythagoras showed that through patterns and ratios, numbers expressed themselves in musical harmony as well. One day he heard blacksmiths working with four bars of metal. He noted that three of them sounded good together, but the fourth bar was discordant. Pythagoras had the blacksmiths exchange hammers, but the tones remained the same. The only difference among them was their length. The three bars were inversely proportional to each other, consequently making a chord. The fourth discordant bar was not, which accounted for it being out of tune. From that flash of understanding, Pythagoras developed a theory of harmonics which grew to encompass everything from architecture to the movement of our planets.

Mainstream Greeks saw Pythagoras and his fanatical long-haired Pythagoreans as a subversive cult. The "filthy vegetarians" preached reincarnation in human or animal form. Pythagoras claimed that Hermes had provided the gift of remembering prior incarnations, including life as Aethalides, the son of Hermes. Pythagoras once reportedly stopped a man from beating a dog whom Pythagoras recognized as an old friend.

After his death, the Pythagorean schools were crushed and burned and their followers killed. Only the initiates that fled the country survived, but his Pythagoreans were already infected with their teacher's zeal. He was the first man in history to record, experiment and measure natural laws. Pythagorean schools had communal ownership, so it comes as no surprise that much of his early followers' work may have been attributed to Pythagoras. Many great scientists, including Galileo, Kepler and Descartes built their theories from Pythagorean thought. His immense theories are still being proven today, many of which could never have been validated during his own lifetime. Pythagoreans were the first to conceive of atoms, quantum physics and an accurate law of gravitational theory – all of which were not scientifically proven until the last century. His influence still has profound impact on the contemporary world.

Today we know some of the "discoveries" of Pythagoras were not his, but received in those traveling years or attributed to him by his followers. Nevertheless, the superb scientist/mystic was the candle that shed the light of ancient knowledge throughout the darkness of the world.

– NIALLA

WATER RITES OF FIJI

THE THREE HUNDRED thirty-three islands of Fiji float the South Pacific in various patterns. Some groups appear as if someone dropped dozens of islands in a hurried escape. Others are arranged as if placed during a moonlight dance. Fiji was born and raised in some of the deepest waters of the South Pacific Ocean. The nature of the sea has influenced the culture and spirit of the inhabitants, who populate over one hundred thirty of the islands. The language tone is as melodic as the waves. Locals speak to the large body of water through various water rituals. The sacramental requests tend to focus on bonding, thanking, awakening, pleasure, forgiveness, appreciation for food, for life. Money and success don't tend to be addressed.

I grew up on a farm on the banks of the largest river. For me and my Indian family, life stirred at sunrise. I woke up hearing the brass bells from my grandmother praying under the hundred-year-old mango tree. As I gulped my warm milk, I heard the distant blast of the conch signaling the safe return of the fishermen. It came from a village about a mile away, and I ran barefoot toward the sound.

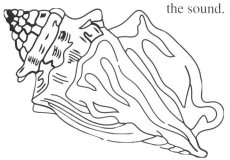

At the beach, a tall Fijian draped in a *sulu* at his waist held a large conch shell in both hands. He was the Mataqali, the head of the village. Facing the ocean, up to his knees in water, he blew strong, deep sounds. The villagers crowded the beach, scanning the horizon for the boat. After a series of long blows, the Mataqali spoke to the ocean passionately, in a warriorlike manner. Anyone not knowing this water ritual could mistake him for yelling at the sea. But he was thanking the ocean, seeking continued insight for its care, and expressing appreciation for the experiences it provided. The Fijian then bent down and filled the large conch with sea water. He lifted it ceremoniously and then slowly poured it back, loudly addressing the ocean with words of love and fear. When the boat touches sand, smiles light up the eager faces of the villagers.

Fiji's spirituality is embedded in the elements of nature herself. The two distinct cultures, Indian and Fijian, have many similarities, including their reverence for water.

Every year after the hurricane season, the local pundit performs the water ritual in preparation for the firewalking ceremony. The participants are either in the process of healing or simply in quest of inner strength.

Water harnesses fire. The twenty-one-day event begins with all participants staying together at the temple and following a strict practice of meditation, silence and prayer. The diet consists of simple vegetarian foods. The twentieth day, always a Saturday, the celebrants reach the peak of their meditations leading into a trance. They also prepare big hardwood logs for burning and making hot coals for the following day.

Early Sunday morning, the group gathers to begin the seven-mile walk to the river for the main water ritual preceding the fire-walking ceremony. Hundreds of people follow to witness the water service. The would-be firewalkers are roped in; they are slowly getting into a deep trance and the rope keeps them together. As they approach the river, the firewalkers grow intense with energy, hopping and spinning like dervishes. They all run into the water and submerge over and over as they sway in a trance. When ready, each approaches the priest, who drives sutures into several parts of the body; cheeks, chin, chest, forehead. Then the priest puts a small lime in the mouth of the firewalker

and sutures the cheeks, driving through the lime. When all the firewalkers have experienced these preparations, the priest chants and pours buckets of water over each participant. The water represents the element that will harness the fire and cleanse the firewalker of all distraction, ensuring that the experience will be free of burns or pain.

The crowd gets thicker. The firewalkers are now fully in a trance and start the return to the temple for the walk across the coals that have been burning for twenty-four hours. The priest returns with them, carrying a bucket of water mixed with turmeric and a *neem* branch. Along the way he splashes the firewalkers to keep them in a trance.

The ritual leads the individuals' psyche to the true nature of water. They become water, their bodies sway like waves, fire doesn't burn them because now they are water.

– Sunita Dutt

The Spirit of Anointment

THE WORLD IS FULL of wonders, each vibrating to its own special harmony. By working with these spirits of nature, a witch can effect aspects of magic. To prepare for an anointment, the practitioner selects an oil, ointment or similar substance to reflect the properties of the work at hand. An incantation is chanted over the substance, saturating it with intent. Then, when the time is right, a witch uses it to anoint the body or an object.

Anointing is a form of sympathetic magic in the belief that the supernatural properties of a natural object can be conferred from one to another through proximity. The theory that everything in the world has its own vibration, which can be instilled and passed on to another, is not new. Recent scientific investigations have confirmed that intent has an effect on water crystal formations. Magnets function based on the alignment of molecules in metal.

Cultures all around the world use incantations and consecrations. Saying words of power over a mixture endows it with aspects to be used subsequently. In *The Lore of the Unicorn*, Odell Shepard illustrates how sympathetic magic works: "The Stellion, which is a beast like a Lyzard, is an enemy to the Scorpion, and therefore the Oyle of him, being purified, is good to anoint the place which is stricken by the Scorpion."

Ancient rituals

Anointings have a colorful history. The early practice in West Africa occurred when men rubbed themselves with lion fat to increase courage. Egyptians anointed their idols and altars with ointment included in their sacred offerings. Early Hindu and Christian myths abound in accounts of kings and generals being anointed with *ghee* (purified butter) before they could take office. The Roman emperor Vespasian is said to have restored a man's sight by anointing his eyes with spittle. Even the Greek goddess Demeter practiced anointing. When she chose to make Demophon immortal, Demeter rubbed him with ambrosia. The goddess continued the magic by breathing on him softly and clasping him to her bosom. To finalize the spell, Demeter thrust him harmlessly into the fire of the hearth. Proceedings stopped abruptly when Demophon's mother began to scream with fear.

Using the sympathetic magical characteristics of oil was not beyond the

Christian church, either. Gregory of Tours reported one bishop setting oil on St. Martin's tomb to infuse it with the saint's essence. And in 813 AD, the Council of Mainz warned priests to keep close watch over their holy oil to prevent it being used in sorcery rites. This was an about-face from earlier times when priests used the "chrism" to undermine pagan practices.

The oil base used in anointing ointments is significant, and through the ages often had cultural connections. There were deities in Egypt, Sumeria, Babylon, Greece and India that specifically governed sacred trees such as the olive, almond and varana. The holy oil in the Old Testament called for a base of olive oil mixed with myrrh, cinnamon, fragrant cane (interpreted as calamus or cannabis) and cassia.

Flying ointment consists of various herbs that witches rubbed from heel to head to induce astral travel, sometimes in the shape of a bird. Some of the traditional mind-altering ingredients included aconite, belladonna, datura, mandrake, henbane, hemlock and foxglove – all highly toxic. Other constituents were difficult to find and unsavory to even contemplate, such as the blood of a bat. The finger used to anoint can be symbolic as well. Egyptians used the little finger of the right hand. In Italian folk tradition, to avert the evil eye women used their middle finger to apply spittle and dirt to the foreheads of children. The Catholic church, however, employs the thumb as the finger of power in baptisms. For usage by the adept, the key to anointing is a focused intent and using a medium that best suits the purpose at hand. Water is

wonderful for transferring healing, nurturing, emotional and psychic properties. For more earthly pursuits, olive oil or almond oil have been used for thousands of years. Oil is also a great base for a fertility anointing, as is breast milk or semen.

The preparation

To perform an anointment, you can infuse oil and water with herbs, roots, flower essences, resin or stones. Making your own oil is most effective, as it aligns with your personal spirit through the process. But purchasing oil for this purpose also works, although synthetics should be avoided. Many adepts like to add several drops of essential oils to an oil base. The natural properties in the substances are of the highest importance. The herbs for anointment should

ACONITUM
also known as Wolfsbane or Monkshood

correspond magically to the working at hand with elemental and specific properties, easily ascertained in herbals and magical books. Often their common names clue us to their uses: "self-heal," "heart's ease," "witches torch." Nicholas Culpeper and other early herbalists were careful in assigning the zodiacal correspondences to these plants, as zodiacal influences were the base of early healing practices. Herbs should be gathered during an efficacious time. Traditionally herbs gathered in the morning are most potent. However, a full moon harvest will increase lunar properties as the hours between dawn and noon bring solar increase.

Once you have your basic ingredients, add twice as much of the herb, powdered bark or flower as oil. Let them sit in a warm place for up to two weeks or for a magically significant period of time. After steeping, strain the oil through a cheesecloth. If the scent is not sufficiently strong, repeat the process. Some practitioners add coloring and stones to further increase the properties of the anointment. Two lodestones are commonly added to increase magnetic forces.

To make strong water-based herbal extracts for anointments, the plants are boiled in just enough water to cover for twenty minutes. Cool and re-boil the water with a fresh batch of herbs. After filtering the herbs, the solution can be boiled down further to a concentrated amount. This is a quick method of creating an anointing fluid, but must be used readily as it will not store well. This liquid can be made into a condenser by mixing it with distilled alcohol. Alcohol, or *aqua vitae*, the "water of life," literally increases your anointment's spirits and storage time as well. Condensers should be stored in the refrigerator. Franz Bardon, the Czech occultist, recommended adding a gold tincture to condensers to increase their powers. Spittle or blood will also increase the fluid's life force.

To boost the power of an anointing even further, a charm can be recited during the application process. Amulets, talismans and mojo bags are well suited to anointing. Clothes and the human body also serve well in keeping the power with you. The chakras, the doorways to the senses (eyes, ears, nose, mouth) and the hands and feet are good power spots to anoint. Many ancient anointings applied the unction to the eyes, the top of the head or over the entire body. The oils, herbs and similar natural benefits offer the gift of anointment, a time-honored ritual that emanates magic.

– NIALLA

Leap of Wisdom

Keep your thoughts positive because your thoughts become your words.
Keep your words positive because your words become your behavior.
Keep your behavior positive because your behavior becomes your habits.
Keep your habits positive because your habits become your values.
Keep your values positive because your values become your destiny.

– GHANDI

Anne Rice – A Queen of Witch Tales

"THOSE WHO WOULD have known are already dead," said Anne Rice with an enigmatic smile. The celebrated author of *The Vampire Chronicles* and the *Mayfair* books was autographing a copy of *The Witching Hour* as she spoke. It was 1991 at a bookstore near Disney World in Orlando, Florida. Rice confirmed her birthday as October 4, 1941, in New Orleans, the background for many of her stories. Then she turned her attention to the next in the line that stretched around the block. Each person was holding a cherished first edition to be signed. A funereal black stretch limo was parked out front, magicians entertained the eager crowd, and fans offered bouquets of wilted and dying roses. Many wore black to honor the adored writer, usually wearing a black turtleneck sweater with a skirt or slacks in the same midnight hue. Anne Rice is a Libra, born just before the Moon was full as it moved toward a conjunction with Mars in Aries. The Aries planets opposing her Libra Sun suggest energy and innovation. The Sun is sextile Pluto, the planet of darkness and the afterlife. A major influence in the American Goth genre, Rice is most often admired for her fantasy and horror works. In

1976 she published *Interview with a Vampire*, which became an immediate bestseller. Her Mercury, the writer's planet, and her Venus, indicator of love and pleasure, are both in Scorpio, sign of the extremes and passions. Her late husband, the poet Stan Rice, once dismissed the sadomasochistic themes in her novels as "the romantic fantasies of a Catholic schoolgirl."

Rice was the second child born to a large bohemian and free-spirited Irish family. Her parents named her Howard Allen O'Brien, believing that name would bring their daughter fame and fortune. Although she changed Howard to Anne in childhood, Rice has certainly found fame and fortune. Films and a Broadway play with a television series in the planning stages have been inspired by the mystical characters that she created. The sheer volume of her work, over forty lengthy novels, fulfills the promise of Rice's natal Jupiter, the planet of growth and expansion, in eloquent Gemini. Jupiter has a bearing on spirituality and Gemini expresses the nature of duality.

In 1998 Rice returned to Catholicism, the faith of her childhood, and has since become a Christian novelist.

Anne has Type 1 diabetes, and constantly battles her weight. It has ballooned to over 280 pounds at times. She once described herself as "a totally conservative person who came out of the 1960's. I was typing away while everybody else was dropping acid and smoking grass. I was known as my own square." Her Moon Node and

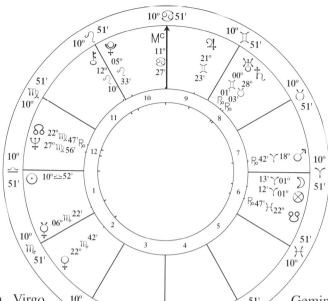

Neptune in Virgo can be linked to her health and work ethic. Anne is eloquent about what it means to lose New Orleans. She encourages support for rebuilding the devastated areas and helping the victims of hurricane Katrina. It is interesting to note that Anne suddenly placed her three New Orleans properties on the market and moved to La Jolla, California, in January, 2005, just months before the hurricane ravaged lives and property in her home city. Her Uranus (ruler of upsets and storms) and Saturn (security base) are conjunct on the Taurus-Gemini cusp. Both planets mutually apply to a benevolent trine aspect to her natal Neptune (indicator of intuition) in Virgo. Did she have some inkling of the disaster that was to come to New Orleans? Did she just make the move to be closer to her son, novelist Christopher Rice?

Perhaps astrology has the answers. Anne Rice's horoscope above may provide more insights into the complex and brilliant individual who has contributed so much to the world of the modern witch.

– Dikki-Jo Mullen

Anne O'Brien Rice

October 4, 1941, New Orleans

(Sunrise Equal House chart used, as the exact birth time is unrecorded.)

Sun – 10 Libra 52, Moon – 1 Aries 13, Mercury – 6 Scorpio 22,
Venus – 22 Scorpio 42, Mars – 18 Aries 42 (retrograde), Jupiter – 21 Gemini 23,
Saturn – 28 Taurus 03 (retrograde), Uranus – 0 Gemini 01 (retrograde),
Neptune – 27 Virgo 26, Pluto – 5 Leo 33, Moon's North Node – 22 Virgo 47

 # Wicca and Christianity

A personal perspective

Dr. Hans Holzer has written an amazing number of books, the box score over one hundred forty at last count. America's leading parapsychologist, Holzer has spent decades writing about apparition theories and his investigations into haunted locations. Holzer has also written thirteen novels dealing with paranormal phenomena, including the popular Amityville books and films. Born in Vienna in 1920, Holzer received a doctorate in comparative religion with a speciality in parapsychology from the London College of Applied Science. He has been active for decades as a film writer, TV writer and host, professor and lecturer.

Dr. Holzer and Almanac editor/publisher Theitic are old friends. Last spring they met in New York, and Hans provided us with a wide-ranging update on his beliefs, sometimes "explaining the unexplainable."

LONG BEFORE Christianity arose worldwide, the "Old Religion" dominated the sacred practices of mankind. Sometimes known as "Wicca" or "the Craft," what is new today is the number of new followers disenchanted with the accepted traditional religions. What troubles young people most is the path of power and greed evidenced by certain Christian sects, leaving their adherents feeling spiritually unfulfilled. These new seekers of the Old Religion also evidence concern about deviation from teaching allegedly based on the life and resurrection of Yeshua ben Joseph, otherwise known as Jesus Christ.

Since the discovery of the Dead Sea Scrolls, dating from 200 BC, we know that this remarkable man was a rabbi, a preacher trained in an Essene college of Quram with teaching similar to early Christianity. The Sermon on the Mount and the Beatitudes, two mainstays of Christianity, actually were written about 150 BC and Jesus learned them at Quram. But Christianity was based on much more than these teachings, important as they are. The miraculous Resurrection after he had been crucified by the Romans is a key belief. That his physical death was achieved is beyond doubt. A centurion, feeling sorry for the suffering of Jesus on the cross, pierced his heart with a lance, assuredly a fatal injury.

No doubt exists that witnesses saw Jesus alive in a body after the crucifixion. But what appeared to his wife Mary Magdalene and to his disciples on the road to Damascus was certainly his etheric body, which I understand in this

---

Above left: Pentacle Flower. Flower and star together indicate heaven and earth.
Above right: Spiritu Santo, the third aspect of the Christian Trinity.

way: We are born with a double body, the physical form derived either from our parents or grandparents, the Mendelian Law. But from another source, the waiting line of those desiring to be reincarnated, a suitable spirit is selected and instilled in us at the moment of birth. The myth of physical resurrection, truly a miracle if it had occurred with the outer physical body, is the basis of the Christian religion. After crucifixion, the power of Jesus to heal the sick and his appearance in the etheric inner body were considered "miracles" – which they were not. The disappearance of the crucified body was also considered a "miracle." But the body of Jesus was simply placed by his followers into the empty tomb of Joseph of Arimathea and later removed to the Church of the Holy Sepulcher in Jerusalem, where it remains. But Wicca, the Old Religion, does not perform miracles. The effective spells adherents sometimes enact, for good or evil, are not miracles – they depend on the believer and the emotional energy generated.

What Wicca brings to the table, so to speak, is a great knowledge of natural law, an understanding of healing and herbal remedies, and an emotional involvement with collective rituals, including community dancing. The coven joins as one to raise energy mentally, often sending it forth to heal someone either in the circle or at a distance. To people untrained in such practices favorable results sometimes seem "miraculous," although they are merely natural.

Wicca is not a mystery religion, but what people practiced under many names in various parts of the world. The Mother Goddess, the primary divinity, is purely symbolic. It denotes that the practice is female oriented, whereas the Christian religion is dominated by the male and really denigrates female aspects. The universe we know consists of both genders, and the coven recognizes the duality with a priestess and high priest, each ruling for half a year. A deep sense of belonging occurs among members of a coven. But the Halloween stories about witches flying through the air on broomsticks are fantasies, derived from an ancient May Day ritual. At that time riding around a field on a broomstick supposedly encouraged the crop to grow to the height of the broomstick.

The Witches' Almanac tells its readers many things about the seasons and what works best at certain dates. There is, after all, nothing in this universe that is supernatural – only natural laws not fully understood.

– HANS HOLZER

Maryland Moon and Water Lore

SEVERAL FOLK beliefs in Maryland traveled across the Atlantic with colonists and immigrants from the British Isles and Europe. Often regional lore represents smatterings of magical theory. According to Maryland watermen, "The best time to eat hard crabs is during a waning moon – that's when they have the most meat. Soft crabs are most plentiful and are tastiest during a full moon." The crab, as a water animal, often links to the moon, as do other shellfish. And as for many convictions about moon influence, sexual theories arise. The claw of a Chesapeake blue crab is allegedly a fertility charm, and some say its meat is an aphrodisiac. The phallic nature of a crab claw makes it a fertility charm, as well as a guard against the evil eye.

"It is bad luck to whistle on the deck of a boat," an old maritime belief declares. In doing so you might inadvertently whistle up a windstorm, as witches were often accused of doing.

In Dorchester County, some people attest that it is a good thing to sing while catching oysters, although they don't say what song. Presumably your concert can petition the water spirits (undines, nymphs, sprites) for a good oyster catch, whatever the success level of your voice.

If you are sailing on the Chesapeake and the wind is still, you can try "buying a wind." All you need to do is toss a penny overboard and a breeze should come right along. This folk practice is

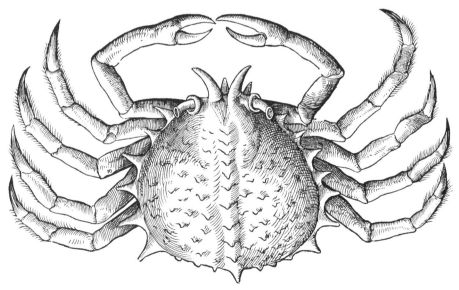

another petition of the sea spirits, alert to a variety of offerings.

"In winter, a ring around the moon means it will snow." The ring around the moon in winter is formed by its reflection of ice crystals in the air, so it reasonably could predict snow.

Sometimes folklore is preserved in old verses:

> *Who will draw a ring around*
> *the moon?*
> *Who will draw a line from*
> *star to star?*
> *Who will sing a penny worth*
> *of song?*
> *To tell them how in love we are?*

Sometimes counting stars provides information. "The number of stars in the circle around the moon tell the number of days before a storm will come," we are assured.

"When the horns of the moon point down, it will rain." People once believed that the moon holds water because of its association with the tides. So "when the horns of the moon point down," the pail is upside down and the water spills.

"Plant all underground crops on the dark of the moon for a better yield." Underground crops, such as potatoes, are hidden crops and are associated with the time when the moon is hidden, that is, the dark of the moon. Much gardening lore in Maryland as well as the rest of America is associated with the moon, because it is believed to govern growth. Some gardeners advise you to transplant or graft above-ground annuals during the waxing moon.

"Make soap on the increase of the moon. It will thicken better." Making soap is no longer much of a practice, but it conforms with the conviction that the waxing moon aids growth or increase of any kind. Another folk belief asserts that if you cut your hair during the waxing of the moon it will grow back rich and full.

"Take an old, dirty penny, rub it on your warts, then throw it over the right shoulder, facing a full moon, and the warts will go away." We hope you don't have any use for this one.

– MYTH WOODLING

Dharamsala
Tibet in Exile

SURVIVORS OF A decades-long exodus, Tibetans have set about reweaving the threads of their ancient culture in many lands, most notably Dharamsala in Northern India. This former summer retreat for British officers in the foothills of the Himalayas has become a center for Tibetan culture, language and spirituality. The site is also the seat of the Tibetan government in exile and home of that country's temporal and spiritual leader, the fourteenth Dalai Lama.

The culture of Tibet is a complex mix of Nepali, Chinese and Indian Tantric Buddhism with Bon, a synthesis of local shamanistic practices. Bon adherents provide access to the powers of the land, water and sky through a system that is now widespread. Although Tibetan legend tells of Bon being brought to Tibet by a supreme adept named Tonpa Shenrap, it is likely that the religion evolved with and from indigenous clan traditions.

Buddhism itself has mingled with Bon and taken a unique Tibetan form, with art and iconography that is instantly recognizable. Legend places the formal arrival of Buddhism in the seventh century with the unification of Tibet under King Songtsen Gampo, whose two wives – one Nepali and one Chinese – were Buddhists. Buddhism became the state religion, although Gampo took care not to suppress the Bon tradition. One of the first great Tibetan Buddhist teachers, Padmasambhva, was an Indian sage who had been initiated by Tantric *dakinis*, female spirits sometimes embodied as human women. This factor introduced an esoteric current of Buddhism linked to "inner" teachings by the Buddha for gaining enlightenment quickly. Although the dominance of Buddhism and Bon has shifted back and forth several times over the centuries, Buddhism currently prevails as the country's primary spiritual tradition. The traditional rivalry has eased with time and many modern Tibetans practice both religions.

The Indian sanctuary
China and India, as Tibet's closest neighbors, have both culturally influenced Tibet. The 1949 invasion by communist China placed Tibetan culture under threat, since communism views all forms of religion as false and dangerous. Ten years after the Chinese invasion of Tibet, the Dalai Lama Tenzin Gyatso was forced to flee. Disguised as a refugee, he managed to cross the border into India after a grueling journey, largely on foot. In 1960 India offered Dharamsala as a settlement for

Tibetans fleeing the communist regime. The area is not far from the ancestral home of the Buddha, and was an early center for Buddhist communities until the seventh century AD. A resurgence of Hinduism eventually erased this early history. But the Tibetans, who are largely Buddhists, find spiritual ancestors here, and rich historical sites are waiting to be explored.

In this sanctuary, Tibetans have begun creating their culture anew. The mountain climate is reminiscent of the high mountain scenery of their homeland. Temples, residences and monasteries, many bearing the names of places left behind in Tibet, have been rebuilt here. People wear traditional garments, while the smell of *momo* (meat dumplings), butter tea and barley beer waft from shops and homes, accompanied by traditional songs, both sacred and secular.

Monastic and cultural centers host complex and beautiful ceremonies, operas and dances – the center of Tibetan life for centuries. When he is not traveling and educating elsewhere in the world, the Dalai Lama teaches publicly and works toward the peaceful liberation of his homeland. He was awarded the Nobel Peace Prize in 1989.

Many circumstances have changed with the exodus of Tibetan culture from its homeland. The Dalai Lama has emphasized the importance of women in Buddhist tradition. Several nunneries have been founded or are under construction, reversing a centuries-long trend. Secular women also have greater opportunities for spiritual practice and study here. A great effort is also being made to extend basic education to all children in the community, with money raised worldwide for schools. And Tibetan traditions – for over a thousand years kept secret in the heart of Tibet's forbidding mountains – have become available to all worthy students willing to undertake these strenuous disciplines.

At the center of this city of eight thousand refugees rises Namgyala, a memorial dedicated to those who have lost their lives in the struggle for a free homeland. Tibetans come here to spin prayer wheels and recite mantras. The devotees are a living reminder of how the broken strands of a rich culture can be rewoven with diligent effort and great compassion for all beings, including one's enemies.

– ELIZABETH ROSE

A Splendid Staff

Caduceus (Swiss, 1515)

ALCHEMISTS consider it the union of the sun and moon. One of the oldest tarot decks, the Marseilles, displays it on the Two of Cups. Magical orders see it as a symbol of balanced spirit and the union of the four elements. Most, however, recognize it as a symbol of the medical profession.

Our common image of the caduceus is a rod entwined by two serpents and mounted with a winged globe or bird. It symbolizes gaining the light of wisdom by descending into the underworld and returning. It is the wand of a shaman, a shepherd's crook, the trunk of the World Tree. It represents finding balance between polarities. Snakes coil around it three-and-a-half times in a double helix like the serpent-fire, *ida* and *pingala*, which rise about the *shushumna* (or spine) in kundalini yoga. The caduceus has been used to symbolize commerce, healing, thieves, knowledge of secret mysteries, neutrality and the herald who delivers messages. On first glance, there doesn't seem to be any order to its meaning, but through an examination of the deities that have wielded the symbol, its meaning is revealed.

Most people think of the caduceus as associated with Hermes or his Roman counterpart, Mercury. It has been used by other deities, such as Ishtar, Pax, Cybele, Felicitas, Anubis, Minerva, Nemesis and Tanit – but always by invoking the powers of its primary owner. The tale of Hermes, the friendliest god to man, is linked to the caduceus, or *kerykeion*. Born in a cave like a snake, the deity knows the mysteries of the underworld. He has all the powers of the "chaotic night": cunning, cattle thievery, bringing dreams and fertility. Hermes uses these capacities to steal Apollo's cattle and hide them in a cave. When Apollo, the sun god, takes offense, he brands Hermes "comrade of the dark night." Their Olympian father, Zeus, puts Hermes to work as a shepherd, a merchant and a messenger to keep him out of trouble. From a Homeric Hymn to Hermes, a crucial moment occurs when Apollo befriends Hermes, granting him the staff:

> *I will give you a splendid staff*
> *of riches and wealth: it is of gold,*
> *with three branches, and will keep*
> *you scatheless, accomplishing*
> *every task, whether of words or*
> *deeds that are good.*

Like the ascending snakes on his wand, Hermes' ingenious reptilian mind was called out of the chaotic world of the unconscious to a higher purpose.

Serpents have not always been coiled around Hermes' wand. Early on the symbol depicted an olive branch wrapped with two white ribbons. Mythology tells us that Hermes gained the snakes in his role of mediator by making peace between a pair of fighting snakes that then coiled around his wand as if mating.

With his caduceus Hermes could awaken souls or put them to sleep, living or dead. In his role of "laying unspotted souls to rest" Hermes guided the dead to the underworld, receiving the honorific "The One Who Leads Souls Away and Back Again." In a Greek depiction of Hermes summoning the dead, his *kerykeion* has a single coiled circle of two serpents that form horns atop it like the astrological symbol for Mercury. These early caducei often had the wings placed below the horned head, creating the planetary symbol for Mercury.

The symbol was carried by secret societies, heralds (indicating neutrality) and merchants on trading expeditions to communicate their nature. Roman legions displayed the caduceus where their "caduceators" or heralds were in battle to indicate their status

as noncombatants. In this spirit the U. S. Army Medical Corps adopted the caduceus in 1902. But the Rod of Aesclepias, a cypress wand coiled with only a single snake, seems more appropriate for the medical profession – Aesclepias was the Greek god of healing.

The symbol appears in many other ancient cultures, including Babylonian. Around 4000 B.C., the caduceus was wielded by the god Ningishzida. In animal form Ningishzida was depicted as a horned winged serpent with four feet. In human form he has two serpents resting on his shoulders. Like a snake ascending from the underworld, his divine serpent-fire was the "bread and water of life," able to perform magic and healing. Ningishzida's hieroglyphic is used synonymously with the Tree of Life, which some mythologists believe is the staff around which the snakes are coiled. The same god turns up on the earliest caduceus, a cuneiform representing the Ningishzida as a bulbous staff entwined with two snakes in a double helix, similar to DNA. Other hieroglyphics depict the snakes as recognizably male and female, often with a bird resting on top. Portrayed as male or female, Nin-gish-zida, or "Lord of the Good Tree," is an early Assyro-Babylonian vegetation deity, probably of a fruit tree. Like

Roman termini. *Mercury is standing upon the globe, with cap and wings attached to the head and wings to the feet, the center filled with the caduceus.*

Early Sumerian version of the Caduceus

its skin, the snake has come to signify rebirth and eternal life or a sudden and painful death that a bite can bring.

Having first been recorded by the Assyrians, the winged globe is used by magical orders as a representation of the sun. The winged globe is reported to represent the 33rd and highest degree of Masonry. The Rosicrucians interpret it as the perfected soul returning to its source.

The caduceus teaches us moderation – the balance between light and dark. It is the path of mankind growing out of unconscious existence into a higher awareness. It is also the way of the shaman who gains the light of wisdom by first knowing the mysteries of the underworld.

NIALLA

a tree, he guards and guides the underworld where he retrieves life force. Also known as "The Great Serpent of Heaven," Ningishzida branches to the sky and is associated with the constellation Hydra. Some early caducei representing him portray the two snakes as visibly male and female – emblems of balance. They also symbolize life, death and renewal, health, wisdom, cunning and libido. Tammuz, the other guardian to the underworld, is a date-palm deity who also assumes serpent form and may be an aspect of Ningishzida. Together they mediate between mankind and the god Anu. Some biblical scholars believe Ningishzida metamorphosed into the Garden of Eden's serpent in the tree. In "Adapa and the South Wind," the god Anu has Tammuz and Iszida (Ningishzida) offer the bread and water of life to Adapa. Upon his lord Ea's direction, Adapa refuses it. Anu discloses that in the act of denying himself heavenly nourishment, Adapa has refused the gift of immortality. Immortality has long been associated with serpents. In the shedding of

Aesculapius
From a Florentine statue

126

BOOKS

The Mystery Traditions: Secret Symbols and Sacred Art by James Wasserman, Destiny Books, paperback, 147 pp., $19.95 (U.S.), $24.30 (Canada).

THIS PROFUSELY illustrated volume offers a dazzling variety of imagery. The diversity of the graphics does more than any "text only" could do to enrich our understanding of the Western mystery traditions. The book is an excellent source of knowledge about a wide range of occult subjects – astrology, cosmology, Kabbalah and the Tree of Life, initiation, magick and the gods, sexuality, alchemy, tarot decks, symbolist and visionary art, and secret societies (an addition to this revised volume). The majority of the illustrations are in excellent color. Most of the images have been previously published, but the scope of this assemblage is unique. The reader has in one place a multiplicity of potent images, any one of which could serve as a focus for meditation.

Each chapter includes a short introduction, four pages or less, of that section's material. And each illustration appears within its time period of the text, although these depictions transcend any such limitations.

It is difficult to find words to describe this work. The images derive from so many periods and locations; the writing in the introductory sections is so profound and so succinct; the overall impression is so overwhelming that I feel the book should be read a little at a time. To attempt to comprehend all the rich contents at one or two sittings does a disservice to the work and to yourself. Take the time to allow the images in the book to work for you. Permit them to stimulate new thoughts and inspire changes both in how you perceive yourself and the wider world. The benefits you reap may astonish you.

The Mystery Traditions: Secret Symbols and Sacred Art is one of the most stunning works I have seen in a very long time. The combination of such excellent quality and such a reasonable price is a pleasant surprise. If you are interested in symbolic representations of mystical themes, this book belongs in your library. Be assured that you will enjoy and savor the volume again and again over the years.

– MIKE GLEASON

From a Witch's Mailbox

Dear Editor: My heart goes out to all of you. I am so sorry to hear about the passing of Elizabeth Pepper. For many years I have enjoyed *The Witches' Almanac* and her unique sense of artistic style. Elizabeth's passing will be felt by her admirers throughout the world, while her gracious gifts will long be treasured.

– Maureen
Salt Lake City, Utah

Thank you for your kind words. The Almanac staff has been enormously touched by the beautiful expressions of condolences from so many of our read- ers. We wish we could answer every one, but the volume of mail has been overwhelming. Be assured that your letter and all others will be treasures in the Almanac archive.

Dear Editor: Will you be offering for sale any of the illustrations of the cats drawn by Elizabeth and illustrated on her Memoriam page? I would like to get a print of the black cat at the top and a different one for someone else.

– G.G.
e-mail

Yes, we also intend to establish a gallery of prints, which will certainly include Elizabeth's beautiful drawings. We have some exciting plans, but this past year the staff has been absorbed in issuing the Almanac you are now reading without Elizabeth's major input. But keep an eye on our website for upcoming news.

Dear Editor: I am writing to offer my sincerest condolences to the friends and family of Ms. Pepper Da Costa. I have been a loyal customer of the Almanac for over ten years and have been lucky enough to receive a lovely handwritten note from her as well as some copies of the first few editions. Absolutely stunning. Her kindness leaped from her letter in a most tangible way.

I so enjoy the Almanac and am delighted that you plan on continuing the tradition. I am also happy to see the new website.

– M.S.
e-mail

Elizabeth loved being in touch with read- ers. We are also happy about our new website, www.TheWitchesAlmanac.com.

Dear Editor: I'm always thirsting for new reading material and have collected pretty much everything you have published. Any new books coming out soon?

– Matt
e-mail

Yes, we do have several literary irons in the fire, but nothing so far along that announcements would be timely, check out our website in the early winter for our newest publication; it promises to be a delight.

Dear Editor: I have spent the last few days enjoying back copies of the Almanac. They are always fun to read. But I am curious about something. How do you pick the birthday people in the calendar? Do they have any significance beyond their obvious accomplishments? I am thinking of such people as William Butler Yeats, Billie Holliday, Fay Wray, Nostradamus, Lucille Ball, Ben Franklin.

– B.C.
Hamden, Connecticut

We have an uncontrollably quirky staff. Names are not chosen for any particular reason, but we can take a stab at recapitulation. Yeats was a great poet with an interest in the occult; Billie's voice thrills and chills; Fay Wray was a terrific screamer; Nostradamus knew practically everything; Lucille Ball was funny; Franklin flew a kite and published the first Almanac.

Dear Editor: Can you please explain where the "Night of the Watchers" on the calendar came from and how it became associated with June 5th. June 5th is my birthday!

– M. B.
Alberta, Canada

We have had several inquiries about this mysterious date. Elizabeth only mentioned that a friend had uncovered this date while researching rare manuscripts in London some years ago. Although we believe Elizabeth must have known its origin, this is all we can offer at this time. You might research the Watchers where they are first seen in the Book of Enoch – one of the lost books of the Bible.

Readers, thank you for your letters. We may need to edit for clarity or brevity.

TO: The Witches' Almanac, P.O. Box 1292, Newport, RI 02840-9998
www.TheWitchesAlmanac.com

Name_____

Address_____

City_____ State_____ Zip_____

E-mail_____

We love to hear from our readers, either via post office or website. Please send us your name and address so that we can add you to our mailing list of Almanac friends. You will certainly hear from us.

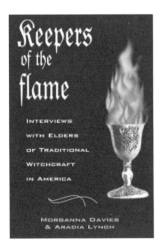

The Koo Hollie Series of Metaphysical Books

by Dikki-Jo Mullen

WELCOME TO FLORIDA'S *Star of the Sorceress School of Metaphysics.*

Practical instruction in Astrology, Tarot, Yoga, Meditation, Ghost Tracking, Spiritual Reading, Past Life Regression and much more is offered in these highly collectible signed and numbered first edition allegorical novels about a Florida astrologer, Koo Hollie. Approx. 200 pages, oversized spiral bound, illustrated with vintage photos and original calligraphy drawings. Adapted from the case books of *The Witches' Almanac* Astrologer and Parapsychologist Dikki-Jo Mullen's professional practice.

Koo Hollie and the Corn Goddess Chronicle

Koo's purchase of the life-sized statue of a mysterious century-old Native American Princess is the catalyst for this intriguing drama. The adventure moves from an ancient beach house on Florida's Space Coast to a cottage in Orlando to the forgotten village of Uponthee in the Everglades. Crime, murder and government corruption develop as the plot unfolds. $22 (please add $3.95 for shipping and handling).

Koo Hollie and the Spirit of Prism Rose

Prism Rose was a beautiful and eccentric young woman who wandered the beaches and streets of Florida's oldest city, St. Augustine, during the roaring twenties. Rose's nickname honored her habit of leaving colored crystal prisms as gifts in unexpected places with little explanation. Nearly a century after Rose's death Koo Hollie finds one of the crystal prisms left hidden in a very haunted Bed and Breakfast. Across time and space Prism Rose influences the re-opening of the case file on a crime long considered cold. $22 (please add $3.95 for shipping and handling).

Crystal Wheel Horoscopes

by Dikki-Jo Mullen

Send your month, day, year, time and place of birth and Dikki-Jo will create a beautiful wooden horoscope plaque with crystals, shells and sharks teeth symbolizing your own astrological placements. Approx. 8" by 10", ready to hang. Hand crafted original. Short interpretation. Astrological symbols and birthstones traditionally are linked to great good luck. $95 (post paid). Order by check or money order and mail to: Dikki-Jo Mullen, PO Box 533024, Orlando, Florida 32853 Please allow about three weeks for delivery by Priority Mail.

Convention Programs, Personal Readings, Group Presentations available.
Phone 407-895-1522 or 321-773-1414.

ARTFROMGREECE.COM

Since 1995, Art from Greece has been offering an eclectic mix of ancient Greek and Minoan art replicas. Our beautiful pottery, frescoes, statues, wall art, and mosaics are all hand made in small family workshops in Greece and imported to our Sarasota, Florida location.

The artists we work with are dedicated to ancient art traditions, and each piece is painted and fired by a single artist over a period of days. In addition, each piece of pottery is Greek terracotta hand thrown on a wheel. Most items on our website have researched information to increase your knowledge and enjoyment of your purchase.

Our goal is to further the appreciation of ancient Greek art and make the fine reproduction work of Greek master artisans accessible to all.

For more information, please contact:

Maria M. Spelleri
and Kosta Koutelias, *Owners*

www.artfromgreece.com
globalme@artfromgreece.com

Our books available by mail order:

A Treasury from past editions...

Perfect for study or casual reading, Witches All *is a collection from* The Witches' Almanac *publications of the past. Arranged by topics, the book, like the popular almanacs, is thought provoking and often spurs me on to a tangent leading to even greater discovery.*

The information and art in the book – astrological attributes, spells, recipes, history, facts and figures is a great reminder of the history of the Craft, not just in recent years, but in the early days of the witchcraft revival in this century: the witch in a historical and cultural perspective.

Ty Bevington, Circle of the Wicker Man,
Columbus, Ohio

Absolutely beautiful! I recently ordered Witches All *and I have to say I wasn't disappointed. The artwork and articles are first rate and for a longtime* Witches' Almanac *fan, it is a wonderful addition to my collection.* Witches' Almanac *devotees and newbies alike will love this latest effort. Very worth getting.*

Tarot3, Willits, California

A Book of Days

By Elizabeth Pepper and John Wilcock   John and Elizabeth celebrate the Seasons of Being with a collection of wise thoughts dealing with all aspects of human life, drawn from every source imaginable – from earliest records to the present, from Aristotle to Thurber. Quotations begin with Spring and Youth, then to Summer and Maturity, on to Autumn and Harvest, then Winter and Rest. Illustrated with over 200 medieval woodcuts.

Magic Charms from A to Z

By Elizabeth Pepper   A treasury of amulets, talismans, fetishes and other lucky objects compiled by the staff of *The Witches' Almanac*. An invaluable guide for all who respond to the call of mystery and enchantment.

Love Charms

By Elizabeth Pepper   Love has many forms, many aspects. Ceremonies performed in witchcraft celebrate the joy and the blessings of love. Here is a collection of love charms to use now and ever after.